The Business of Leadership

Adding Lasting Value to Your Organization

ALAN HOOPER AND JOHN POTTER

Ashgate

Aldershot • Burlington USA • Singapore • Sydney

Ashgate Publishing Limited
Gower House
Croft Road
Aldershot
Hants GU11 3HR
England

Ashgate Publishing Company
131 Main Street
Burlington, VT 05401-5600 USA

Ashgate website:http://www.ashgate.com

Reprinted 1999, 2000

British Library Cataloguing in Publication Data
Hooper, Alan
    The business of leadership : adding lasting value to your
    organization
    1. Executive ability   2. Organizational effectiveness
    I. Title   II. Potter, John
    658.4'092

Library of Congress Cataloging-in-Publication Data
Hooper, Alan, 1941–
    The business of leadership : adding lasting value to your
    organization / by Alan Hooper and John Potter.
        p.   cm.
    Includes bibliographical references and index.
    ISBN 1-85521-753-8 (hb).--ISBN 1-84014-056-9 (pb)
    1. Leadership.   I. Potter, John (John R.), 1947–   . II. Title.
    HD57.7.H68   1997
    658.4'092–dc21

                                                                        96–52272
                                                                        CIP

ISBN 1 85521 753 8 (Hbk)
ISBN 1 84014 056 9 (Pbk)

Typeset by Manton Typesetters, 5–7 Eastfield Road, Louth, Lincolnshire LN11 7AJ, UK.
Printed and bound by Athenaeum Press, Ltd.,
Gateshead, Tyne & Wear.

Contents

List of Figures

Foreword

If you are invited to write a foreword to a book, it is likely that you will agree with much of what the book says, and this is no exception. What, then, should you say about it? It is tempting as a leader of some experience to try to pass on some of that experience, and show how it underlines the lessons that can be learnt from the book. I will not be able to resist the temptation to some degree, but the implication of doing so without qualification is that I have applied these lessons myself throughout my leadership career, in such a way that it has been a progress of unbroken success. Any leader who even implies this is a fraud: we are all human and make lots of mistakes, probably more than others, given the need for leaders to cope with – and, increasingly, to facilitate – change.

I will say at the outset that, to the extent that my career has been successful, it is because I have tried to do, however imperfectly, many of the things in this book. But it will be more fruitful if I first tell you of some of the mistakes that I have made, which illustrate starkly what happens if you deviate from the course that this book sets out.

First, in my impatience, I have often tried to do everything at once. Worse still, I have tried to do all of that by myself. In organizations of any size – in other words, involving more than one person – this is not a sensible way to proceed. It is vital that you should work with and through other people in a spirit of partnership and empowerment. What is more, this has implications for the speed at which progress can be made. If people will not come with you, you are wasting your time: a classic illustration of the old saying, 'more haste, less speed'.

Another cardinal sin I have committed is to lose sight of my vision for the organization from time to time. I can tell you for sure that it was at times like this that things began to go off the rails. In such circumstances, only by firmly restating the vision, and the values that go with it, can you get the organization back on the track.

Blending my own experience with the excellent practical advice given in this book, what is it that really matters in a leader? Some people say that leaders need to be extrovert. I know many successful leaders who are not.

Others say an exceptional intellect is necessary. Of course, you need to know and understand what is going on, but many fine leaders could by no stretch of the imagination be described as intellectuals.

No, what really matters is belief in the vision you have set, in the standards you want to achieve, and, most of all, in yourself. This must be underpinned by a deep trust, both given and received. I do not believe this is possible without a fair degree of humility on the part of the leader, and integrity, both real and perceived, is vital. Leaders must also have considerable courage, to make change where necessary, but, sometimes more importantly, to resist pressure for change where it is unnecessary or inappropriate.

Underneath all of this is the need for the successful leader to have the gift of inner peace, much more likely to be found where you have the support of family and friends – even the greatest and strongest of leaders need this.

If this is what leaders should be, what should they do? You must read the book to answer this question fully, but I would suggest in the barest outline that leaders should take just three steps. The first is to define your vision: what it is you want your organization to be and to achieve. The second is to put the resources, mostly human, in place to achieve this vision. And thirdly, the leader must communicate constantly, not only with the team he has chosen to help him achieve his vision, but also with every constituency that could conceivably have an influence on the success or failure of the organization.

Communication must be constant. It is not something that can be switched on or off at will. It means developing and winning the support of all those around you – coercion simply will not do in the modern age. It is commonplace now for leaders and their motives to be questioned, and leaders must communicate clearly to respond to this. There must be continuous sharing of information; secrecy is the bane of the modern organization and our national corporate culture. And communicating means both learning and teaching: constantly learning as a leader, and teaching those around you how to handle the changes they will confront and how to communicate in turn.

All this and more is in this excellent book. It combines a most interesting review of leadership thought with practical advice. It gives first-class guidance on leadership both for today and for the future. Above all, this book will help leaders at all levels to cope with an ever-changing world of increasing complexity. I commend it to you.

Tim Melville-Ross
Director General
Institute of Directors

Acknowledgements

As with any book, there are so many people who have helped along the way that it is difficult to mention every name. There are some, however, who deserve an extra special mention. First, there are the clients who, over the past ten years, have allowed us to develop our craft through becoming involved with their management training and development programmes. These include ECCI, Eli Lilly & Co, GKN Westland Helicopters, The Wrigley Company Ltd., Sony UK, Philips, Lloyds Bank, Nationwide Building Society, and many others in the private sector. In the public sector, Somerset County Council, Exeter City Council and Caradon District Council all deserve a mention. Although these organizations are very different in the nature of the work they undertake, they all have two things in common: they care about their people and work hard to develop their abilities, particularly in the area of coping with change; and they have all had within them human resource professionals who have been passionate about making a positive difference to the organization. To those individuals, a special thank you is given.

We would also like to thank the Institute of Personnel Development, Results International Plc and Pragmatica International Limited for their support over the past six years, together with all our colleagues associated with the postgraduate diploma and MA in leadership at the University of Exeter, England.

We owe a special debt of gratitude to Professor John Adair for his encouragement and wise counsel. Also we are most grateful to Tim Melville-Ross for his foreword.

Finally, we wish to thank our wives, Jan and Marjorie, for their patience and understanding during the past two years while we have been writing this book.

Alan Hooper and John Potter

1   Why This Book?

Introduction

Leadership is not the same as management. As organizations face up to constant change in an uncertain world, so they are beginning to recognize this distinction, and the essential link between leadership and the management of change.

This book is about leadership: leadership at the top of our organizations and leadership at the front line of our businesses. It is a practical book and its aim is to help the reader to be better equipped to cope with the challenges of today and tomorrow. What has worked in terms of leadership in the past may well be totally inadequate in the future, for there is no doubt that leaders are facing some tough challenges. There is growing pressure on all individuals, particularly leaders, to deliver improved levels of performance. The situation in which most people operate today is becoming more complex, with no clear-cut 'right' answers to problems, and leaders are under greater scrutiny than ever before to deliver what is required of them.

In the past, when so-called 'charisma' and strength of character dominated our concepts of leadership, it was relatively easy for a persuasive individual to influence people through clever rhetoric and emotional appeal. In the modern complex world based on the increasing use of technology, those factors seem less significant. What we are seeing now is a greater emphasis on leadership competence which is more about what leaders *do* than what they appear to *be*. So what do leaders actually do? What is this magical set of attributes and actions which enable an individual to pull people together and achieve extraordinary results?

What Leaders Need to Do

The authors have observed a wide range of leaders across a variety of situations and organizational settings. Effective leaders do certain things which ineffective leaders do not. It is the identification of the necessary set of attributes and the associated actions which is the key to effective leadership and forms the basis of leader competence.

First, leaders set the direction for the enterprise, have a vision of the future which invariably differs from the present and have the ability to communicate that vision both to their team and to the other stakeholders in the enterprise. Second, effective leaders act as powerful examples and role models because they know that people are more influenced by what they see than by what they are told. Third, effective leaders 'walk their talk'; that is, they do what they say they are going to do. As a result of the effective communication of the vision and the way the leader presents himself or herself, followers experience what is best described as an emotional effect. Fourth, if the leader is convincing, the followers will feel they want to be part of the operation and work towards the common goal themselves. This process of orienting people to a common vision is the one of alignment. It is like stroking iron filings with a magnet: people line up and are magnetized by the prospect of the vision becoming reality. As a result of this alignment process, individuals often perform to much higher levels than when operating individually and in isolation.

These four areas form the basis for effective leadership and act as the triggering process for the fifth element: bringing out the best in people. This involves a holistic approach which embraces motivation, empowerment, coaching and encouragement. Effective leaders must also be proactive to create change in order to operate more influentially. They become, in effect, change agents (the sixth competence) and are concerned not just with managing change but also with promoting and facilitating approaches to change so that the organization can progress and develop. This is particularly true for commercial companies competing in the global market-place. The seventh attribute, and a crucial one, is the ability to lead in times of crisis or challenge.

These seven competencies, which are discussed in detail in the book, are the skills required to operate effectively at different levels, in the appropriate style, in order to add value to an organization. This is an important new concept which is associated with the 'business' of leadership. As organizations become leaner and concentrate more on their core activities, so the emphasis on 'added value' has become more focused. This applies equally to the 'profession' of leadership. The fundamental issue about leadership for the future is that it must be oriented more towards developing people and winning their emotional support rather than coercing them and using a position of power to achieve success.

The old-style leader tended to operate out of a strong power base, either through position and rank in the organization or via a dominant personality. As we de-layer our organization, flatten our structures and empower our people, much of the leader's power will become eroded and so, more and more, leaders at all levels will need to be competent at what they do since their decisions are more likely to be questioned in the future. Furthermore, it is not necessarily a high profile or dominant personlity which will be required by the leader of the future; indeed, these attributes alone do not guarantee that an individual will be an effective leader – some of the quieter and more thoughtful individuals have proved themselves very successful at leading others, provided they have had credibility and have gained the respect of their followers.

Leaders of the future will have to be comfortable with the idea of sharing more information with their followers than ever before. In the past, there has been a tendency in organizations for individuals to retain information on the basis that knowledge is power. With the growing impact of information technology on all of our organizations, this information hoarding is simply no longer appropriate.

The leadership dilemma for the future is how to lead people to cope with a dramatically different environment. How do we lead in complex situations where issues are blurred and confused? How do we lead effectively when everyone is being pushed to their limits and is becoming more accountable for their actions? How do we lead effectively when every leadership action is subjected to more scrutiny? How do we lead people whom we never see? Can we lead people who operate at the end of a telephone, fax or computer modem line?

This book sets out to answer these and other significant leadership questions. It addresses the issues and attempts to provide a source of relevant ideas and practical methods for leaders to operate more effectively in these challenging times.

Outline of the Book

The book has been designed to incorporate a logical theme that runs throughout. However, each chapter is self-contained so that the busy reader can concentrate on a specific topic of particular interest.

The next chapter reviews the established opinions on the nature of leadership to enable the reader to understand how leadership theory has developed during the twentieth century. Chapter 3 explores how effective leadership adds value to an organization – what it is that leaders do which really makes a difference and what they will need to do differently in the future.

Virtually every book on leadership advances the power of vision. Chapter 4 addresses the practical aspect, how to create a vision, and it also considers foresight. It explores the technology of neurolinguistic programming to examine how an individual can develop the ability to create and develop effective visions. The technical psychological language is kept to a minimum in the hope that the reader will be able to apply these tools rather than simply read about them.

One of the world's most enduring leadership models is that of the three circles, put forward by John Adair. This model concentrates on the leader operating at three levels: the task, the team and the individual. In the 1970s, the emphasis in business schools and literature was on the task, on management by objectives and hard, bottom-line financial issues. In the 1980s, we saw a change in emphasis towards team aspects. However, the spotlight is about to shift to the individual as more people operate in isolation, with the help of modern technology and communication systems. Chapter 5 thus explores leadership and the individual by considering how the leader needs to cater for the individual in the team and also what an individual requires to do in order to become a competent leader.

Chapter 6 looks at team issues in some depth. The power of an effectively led team can be enormous and it is the leader's ability to tap into this power which is so important. This chapter embraces the training of teams, the use of personality profiling and self-directed work teams, and includes a recipe for success.

In Chapter 7 we distil our thoughts about the seven leadership competencies mentioned above. We believe that these competencies form a basis for effective leadership for the present and the future. The set is adaptive in that it provides a compass by which to navigate in fast-changing, turbulent times. The important thing about these competencies is that they can be developed, indeed they are being taught in a variety of settings, particularly through the work of the authors and their colleagues at the Centre for Leadership Studies, University of Exeter.

In the final chapter we pull together the threads of our argument and point out the way ahead. This includes a 'blueprint' for the future and recommends a continual leadership development programme. We also propose a new concept of 'the learning leader'. In order to be effective, leaders cannot stand still. Like the effective organization, they need to learn, grow and develop continuously if they are to meet the challenges of a constantly changing world.

2   A Review of Leadership Thought

The Starting Point

There is no doubt that leadership is one of the most researched yet least understood aspects of human behaviour. Although theories as to how leaders operate and why some are more effective than others seem to be increasing and expanding at an exponential rate, the problem with much of the published literature is that usually only one or two highly personalized aspects of leadership are considered. In this chapter we present a structured framework designed to act as a reference model to which any specific leadership model may be compared and related. By using this structured core model it is possible to see how the various approaches to leadership relate to each other, leading to more rapid development of individual ability, as leaders at all levels will be in a position to assess their own performance more objectively and be able to alter their approach to leadership challenges as appropriate.

Definitions

The starting point when looking at the theories of leadership is defining the terms we are going to use. If you ask any group of managers or practitioners how they define leadership, you will receive a range of responses. These responses tend to fall into two categories: those focusing on the ability of one individual to influence the actions of others and those focusing on the idea of a group of people being drawn together to work towards a common objective.

If we consider a range of ideas from acknowledged experts in the leadership field, the problem of defining leadership becomes even more challenging. Winston Churchill was once quoted as saying that 'Leadership is the intelligent use of power'. John Adair, of Action Centred Leadership fame, has often described the task of the leader as 'holding people together as a group while leading them in the right direction' (1983). In more flamboyant terms, John Harvey Jones has said that 'Leadership is about getting extraordinary performance out of ordinary people'. What emerges in our minds is that leadership is an emotional rather than an intellectual process, which is perhaps the great attraction and, at the same time, the great frustration of the subject. Here we have a fundamental difficulty for many managers when they look into the subject of leadership, for they usually deny that emotion has any place in business and organizational life. This is a misguided attitude for, if you look at what really makes organizations successful, it is how the people who make up that organization *feel* about their work from day to day.

Leadership is concerned with creating positive feelings on the part of the followers, emphasizing inspiration instead of control, and with unlocking potential rather than issuing demands. It plays a vital role in addition to the management process or, as John Kotter (1990) says, 'Leadership complements management: it doesn't replace it'.

Leaders and Followers

There is an interesting question which we should ask at this stage. Is it possible to have a leader without followers? For example, can a leading portrait painter be a leader in his or her field without some group of admirers which we can label 'followers'? Leadership would seem to reflect the notion of being at the forefront of any activity without there necessarily being any reference to followers. For our purposes in this book, we limit our notion of the nature of leadership to the social process of influencing other individuals in terms of attitudes and behaviour. Before doing this, however, we consider the position of the follower.

What does it take to be an effective follower? Can a leader be effective without being able to act as a follower in some situations? This becomes an interesting issue when you consider some of the more notable leaders in history. In the context of political leadership, the concept of 'followership' is, perhaps, different from what it is in organizations. In many respects, political leaders influence individuals to a way of thinking whereas, in organizations, we are interested in influencing individuals towards behaving in particular ways. In short, political leaders tend to focus overtly on changing beliefs, whereas in organizations we tend to look for behavioural change through covert changes of belief.

Defining Leadership

One of the most comprehensive approaches to trying to define leadership was that undertaken by Ralph Stogdill (1974). He identified over 160 different definitions and categorized them into ten different types. The first of his group of definitions suggests the idea that the leader is essentially the focal point of a group process, like the hub of a wheel, with the individual followers as spokes. The second refers to personality and its effects on the individual followers. This is often called the 'charismatic approach'. On a more sinister level, the third group of definitions presents the idea that leadership is the art of inducing compliance, while the fourth softens this idea to the exercise of influence, which is more socially acceptable.

The fifth group reflects much of the research on leadership carried out in universities in the United States during the 1960s and 1970s, a considerable amount of which looked at leadership performance on the basis of behaviour. As we will see later, even the most complex leadership models can usually be reduced to two aspects of behaviour: task behaviour and relationship behaviour. Many behavioural scientists feel that the only way to assess leadership performance is through the objective analysis of observed behaviour rather than subjective perceptions.

The sixth group of definitions relating to goal achievement has a close link to what many organizations are doing in terms of creating mission and vision statements. The idea of the leader creating a goal or vision to be achieved and then leading the group towards the achievement of that desired situation is a very basic notion of what leadership is all about. The seventh group of definitions relates to the link between leadership and persuasion, which is more subtle than inducing compliance in that the leader influences beliefs and hence behaviour.

The eighth group of definitions refers back to the first, suggesting that leadership is concerned with the effects of interaction between the leader and the followers. The ninth group focuses on the idea of the leadership role being differentiated from the rest of the group, with symbols such as badges of rank, different clothing and so on. The tenth approach considers that leadership involves creating structure in a social system and harnessing resources. In some respects, this tenth group of definitions forms the link between leadership and management which in itself is an interesting issue. In practical terms, many people talk about leaders 'getting a grip on a situation'. This relates to this idea of gaining control, organizing resources, including people, and producing positive outcomes, the basis of what most people call 'management'.

Levels of Leadership

One of the issues which arises frequently during discussions on leadership is that relating to levels of leadership. Is the leadership displayed by the head of state of a country the same as that displayed by a first-line manager in a production plant? There are three clearly defined levels of leadership operation which may be identified in every organization.

First, there is what may be defined as episodic leadership, depicted in Figure 2.1 below. The name is derived from the concept of the social episode identified by Joseph Forgas (1979), a social psychologist who studied the behaviour of individuals in various social settings. Leadership episodes are concerned with a specific task, undertaken by a number of individuals in a limited timescale. Thus the leadership episode is the building-block of leadership development. Leadership episodes may be created quite easily and the operation of either a designated or an emergent leader observed. Leader functions, such as the action-centred approach of John Adair which is discussed later, may be taught and it is frequently possible to produce a positive shift in the behaviour of given individuals in terms of their episodic leadership ability.

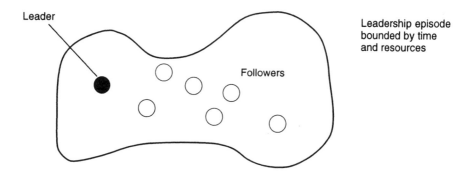

Figure 2.1   Episodic leadership

More difficult to create in terms of training and development situations is the next level of leadership, the ambient leadership situation, shown in Figure 2.2. This is primarily the function of what used to be called 'middle management' and involves creating an environment where leadership epi-

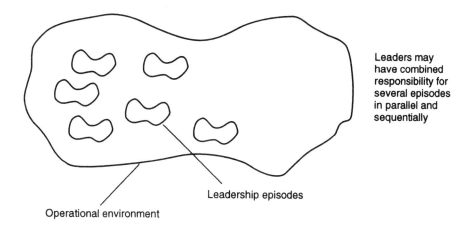

Figure 2.2 Ambient leadership

sodes may take place successfully. It involves creating and promoting a day-to-day culture in the organization which makes it clear which types of behaviour are desirable and which are not. The issue of empowerment is clearly important as regards the ambient leadership situation and it leads to a number of significant questions. Does the organization promote risk taking and innovation or is the emphasis on risk avoidance? Is a considerable amount of energy wasted on interdepartmental squabbles, or is it focused on the organization's mission? Do individuals positively look forward to their involvement in the activities of the organization, or is their input viewed more as a necessary evil required simply to earn a living and maintain their lifestyle?

The third level of leadership is what we might call the strategic leadership level. This is primarily concerned with giving the organization direction, creating a vision or picture of the future of the organization and a mission or purpose in terms of how to bring this vision to fruition. The latter element involves values: what is important is the way in which the organization sets about making the vision reality – in short, the 'price' the organization is prepared to pay for success.

If we consider these three levels of leadership we can see that in the past they have been relatively well defined in our organizations. Manufacturing plants have had first-line supervisors, middle managers and chief executive officers; the army has its sergeants, majors and generals; sales organizations have area sales managers, national sales managers and international sales

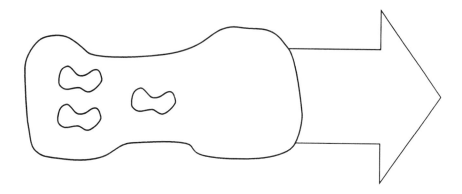

Figure 2.3   Strategic leadership

directors. Leadership is expected to vary according to the level in the organization.

We believe that, in the future, these levels will begin to blur, as they already have done in many organizations, as a result of the removal of layers of management, particularly in the middle of the organization. This process of 'delayering' results in the need for episodic leaders to become more strategic, to see the wider picture of the operation instead of just their own part of the organization. The boards of directors and vice presidents of all of our organizations will need to learn how to operate more effectively as a team if they are going to add significant value to the operation of the organization. In short, as well as strategic leadership skills they will also need episodic leadership skills, to develop their operation as a team, and ambient leadership skills, to create the day-to-day working environment and culture of the organization.

Leadership and Management

We have already suggested that leadership is not the same as management. One of the first approaches to addressing the possible difference is to focus on the emotional aspect of leadership. Corelli Barnett, the noted British military historian observed:

Leadership is a psychological force that has nothing to do with morals or good character or even intelligence: nothing to do with ideals or idealism. It is a matter of relative will powers, a basic connection between one animal and the rest of the herd. Leadership is a process by which a single aim and unified action are imparted on the herd. Not surprisingly it is most in evidence in times or circumstances of danger or challenge. Leadership is not imposed like authority. It is actually welcomed and wanted by the led.

This aspect of the followers wanting leadership is a fundamental issue to any organization or business. Leadership relates to vision, inspiration and emotion rather than control, discipline and logic. An elegant approach to the emotional aspect of the leadership process is the idea that leadership can often be viewed as being transactional or transformational in nature. In transactional leadership, there is an emphasis on a social contract which is a reciprocal relationship between the leader and the followers. In short, the leader gives orders and the followers obey and in return they receive payment in either material or social terms. There is often a negotiation process in operation and the exercise of leadership is dependent upon the willingness of the group to accept the leader.

Transformational leadership is much more exciting. It is frequently associated with values and engages followers so that they are raised to new levels of motivation through what is referred to as 'charisma'. In these situations, the interests of the leaders and followers often become fused and both tend to rise above self-interest and focus on the needs of the group. It could be argued that, in the majority of organizations, transformational leadership is what is most highly sought after. However, in practice, management tends to be transactional in nature. When we consider the difference between leadership and management it is important to recognize both transactional and transformational aspects in terms of the effects on those being managed and led.

In general terms, management is more about maintaining and controlling the status quo, while leadership is more concerned with vision, direction and change. Management often focuses on objectives whilst leadership is concerned with empowerment, inner motivation and values. In essence, leadership is to do with change, vision, direction, aligning people and motivating them through inspiration, whilst management tends to be concerned with controlling complex situations, planning, organizing and problem solving. In his book, *A Force for Change*, Kotter has identified how this may be converted into a working paradigm by focusing on the alignment and inspiration issues for leadership versus the control and predictability aspects for management. He comments that many of the problems currently being experienced by organizations in the West are a result of weak leadership

and strong management. If we can shift the emphasis to both strong effective leadership and management, many of our organizational problems may
well be solved more rapidly.

The qualities approach

The definitions of leadership are of considerable interest in pursuing the
idea of the development of thought on leadership (see Figure 2.4). Early
thought concentrated on the idea of the 'qualities' or 'great man' approach,
which reflects the fact that leadership has been thought of as a primarily
male preserve, largely fuelled by the military influence over the past few
centuries. For many years it was the military world that tended to create the
role models for what most individuals would have described as leadership:
defending or attacking, marshalling and deploying resources, strategy and
tactics, achieving objectives – all this is the language of a traditional view of
leadership.

In the absence of sophisticated social psychological measurement approaches, it was fairly logical that attention to leaders and their ability
would focus on the perceived quality of an individual. Some people had 'it'
(whatever 'it' was) and some did not. The problem is that fairly soon the
'great man' approach to leadership leads to an impasse in terms of identifying effective leaders and how they might be selected and developed, since it
is almost impossible to produce a definitive list of leadership qualities.
While most lists will include some common elements, such as courage,
integrity, consistency and so forth, once the basic set of qualities has been
identified there appears to be an almost unlimited set of supplementary
qualities, all dependent on the nature of the organization. For example,
bishops and military commanders need the quality of courage, but it is hard
to see humility figuring high on the military list, or aggression on the
ecclesiastical.

Even if it were possible to create a definitive list of leadership qualities,
how would the selection process work? If, for example, a robust sense of
humour was agreed upon as a quality, how do you actually select for this
quality? By asking the individual to tell jokes or by watching their reactions
in humorous situations? Even assuming that we could select for a specific
quality, we would then have the difficult task of developing that quality.

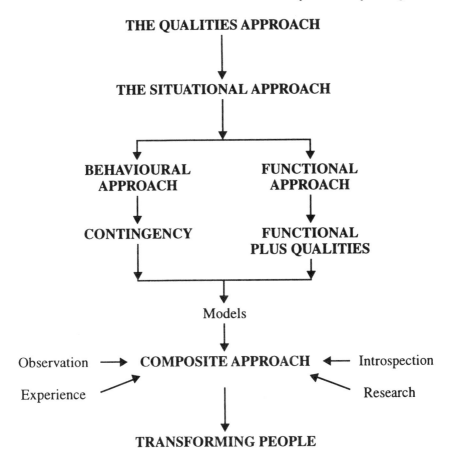

Figure 2.4   Development of thought on leadership during the twentieth century

The Situational Approach

It is this impractical and poorly defined aspect of the qualities approach which led thinkers in the middle of the twentieth century to explore the situational approach to leadership. This was based on the idea that the optimum individual to lead in a given situation was defined by the nature of the situation and the mix of qualities possessed by the individual in relation to the situation. An amusing comment on this approach was the film based on J.M. Barrie's novel, *The Admirable Crichton*, which featured an aristocratic family who became shipwrecked and washed up on an uninhabited desert island. In the early part of the film, the social roles of the head and members of the family and the staff, including the servile butler, are well defined. Once on the desert island, however, the situation changes dramatically and it is the butler who now possesses the necessary knowledge, skills and attitudes to inspire confidence in the followers. As the plot develops, the butler creates an increasing personal power base in terms of this confidence, to such an extent that, some two years after the shipwreck, he has become the governor of the island with the head of the family acting as *his* butler – a total role reversal which highlights firm support for the situational approach, namely that it is knowledge and appropriateness to the situation which will define the most effective leader.

Here we encounter a problem. In most organizations, a specific leader will not handle just one type of situation. In fact one of the key qualities of a leader in an organization is her or his ability to handle a range of situations, most of which are not predicted with any kind of accuracy. We seem to be demanding that our leaders be simultaneously flexible and consistent, with the outcome that leaders appear to be driven by values rather than by qualities or situations. We will return to this issue later in the chapter.

Some Approaches to Leadership Research

It was this frustration with both the qualities and the purely situational approaches that led many researchers in the 1960s to reconsider their thoughts on leadership. In the United States, a number of research projects were undertaken, largely funded by the military. Most of these approaches seem ultimately to reduce to the mixture of task behaviour and relationship behaviour. As part of the Ohio State University Research Studies, Stogdill, whom we have already mentioned in relation to leadership definitions, produced a list of nine leadership behavioural characteristics relating to the various classes of definition: initiation, membership, representation, integration, organization, domination, communication, recognition and production. Through a process of factor analysis, these were reduced to four key areas: consideration for followers; sensitivity to followers and their operation; production emphasis; the initiation of structure.

The first two factors could be conveniently combined as 'concern for people' and the second two factors as 'concern for the task', which is the basis of the task–relationship idea of leader behaviour. This is a consistent theme which seems to emerge from much of the American leadership research. Much of the subsequent research and most of the resultant models talk in terms of some combination of the task and relationship behaviour approach. We will explore several of these models later in this chapter.

The Three Circles Approach of Functional Leadership

While this massive research effort was under way in the United States, John Adair, a military historian at the Royal Military Academy, Sandhurst, had developed an interest in the difference between those officer cadets who seemed to lead well in basic military training situations and those who were ineffective. What was it that effective leaders actually did to gain the support of followers? Adair made an important, innovative move in terms of looking at leadership by analysing the needs of followers rather than concentrating on the way the leader operated. His idea was that leaders should take care of three sets of needs as far as the followers were concerned: needs related to the task, needs relating to the followers, feelings that they are operating as a team and the individual needs of each member of the team. The functional approach to leadership represents these three sets of needs as three circles, with areas of overlap (Figure 2.5).

Figure 2.5   The functional approach

What this model illustrates clearly is that the three areas of leader operation are mutually dependent. If the needs of the task are not satisfied, then the needs of the team and of the individual will also suffer in terms of satisfaction. Individuals may consistently emphasize one or two of the circles at the expense of the third. The model is particularly elegant in terms of its ability to describe actual leader operation and effectiveness.

It also leads us towards the idea of leadership development. The task, team and follower needs are satisfied by the leader carrying out a number of leadership functions, including defining the task, planning, briefing, controlling, evaluating, motivating, organizing and setting an example. It is argued that all these functional areas may be developed with suitable training, thus forming the basis for leadership formation. In terms of leadership research, this was a revolutionary approach because not only did it focus on the followers rather than the leader but it split the 'people' aspect into two parts: the team and the individual.

It is interesting how, over the past 20 years or so, attention in the management literature seems to have focused initially on the task aspects of the leadership and management processes. There was a firm emphasis on hard issues such as financial ratios, management by objectives, discounted cash flow and so on for much of the 1960s, 1970s and early 1980s. The emphasis then seemed to shift towards the effective creation of teams in the workplace, with a considerable amount being written on the positive side of creative effective team structures in organization, although there is very little research evidence to suggest that the team approach is the effective model for all situations. One of the more widely known writers and contributors on the subject of teams is Meredith Belbin, whose team roles approach has attracted considerable interest.

What seems to be happening as we approach the new millennium is a shift towards the individual. A number of commentators, including C.K. Prahalad of the University of Michigan and Sumantra Ghoshal of the London Business School, seem to be pointing towards an emergent recognition that teams will only perform well if the individuals within the team are competent and developing in terms of that competence. Leadership is increasingly being seen as a process created by an individual rather than purely a focus on that individual. If this view prevails, we are indeed in for a fundamental reassessment of the nature of leadership, opening the door for the idea that leadership as a process can be developed at all levels within an organization, from shop floor to boardroom.

Leadership as a Process

There are many reasons why the view of leadership as a process is appealing, particularly now that companies and organizations are operating and competing in global rather than just national or local terms. The focus on an individual tends to be nationalistic at best, which produces problems of national stereotypes. It might be that a manager is reluctant to accept, say, a person of another nationality as a leader in this new global environment simply because they have preconceptions about that nationality. If, however, we can divert attention away from the characteristics of the individual and towards the process they create, we can make progress. The qualities approach was an example of our desire to focus on the characteristics of the individual; what is now required is the realization that it is the process produced *by* the individual which is the important issue.

By taking this idea of leadership as a process we can review some of the current leadership theories and how they might fit into a framework. The qualities approach assumes that the individual possesses qualities which create a process that influences the followers, while the purely situational approach suggests that process is linked to the mix of qualities and their relevance to the situation. Adair's model would suggest that the process is concerned with the satisfaction of the needs of the followers and is aimed at satisfying the three sets of needs in an appropriate mix. If we start to review leadership models from the perspective of the process involved, we can see that the task–relationship model, which just describes leader behaviour without taking into account the impact of that behaviour, is very restricted.

The Work of Fiedler

One novel approach which is based on the task–relationship concept is that proposed by Fiedler in the United States. Fiedler suggests that each individual is predisposed either to a task orientation or to a relationship orientation in varying degrees. Unlike many leadership approaches which try to change the leader to match the situation, Fiedler's approach tries to match the situation to that which the particular leader can best handle. This orientation may be measured using a simple psychological questionnaire, called a Least Preferred Co-worker (LPC) Scale. Essentially, the individual being tested is asked to rate on a set of descriptive scales the person with whom they would least like to undertake a task. If they tend to give that individual positive scores, the suggestion is that the person undertaking the LPC test is more concerned with the relationship than with the task not being performed well. They would thus be awarded a 'high LPC' or relationship-oriented score. If, on the other hand, they tend to rate their least preferred co-worker in terms of negative or low scores on the descriptive dimensions, Fiedler suggests that this represents their unconscious annoyance at the quality of performance of the task being affected negatively by their least preferred co-worker. They would thus attract a 'low LPC' or task-oriented score. The point that Fiedler makes very strongly is that LPC scores tend to indicate a deep-down orientation rather than a day-to-day operational style. He suggests that the LPC is in fact a predictor of the optimum situation involving pressure, stress or lack of control in which the leader finds himself or herself. Fielder suggests that low LPC, or task-oriented, leaders perform more effectively in highly stressful conditions where they are not overconcerned with the feelings of their followers. In addition, they perform well in conditions of low stress, inasmuch as they are not inventing unnecessary work to prove to their superiors or their followers that they are the leader. In short, they can simply 'switch off' and relax. It is at moderate levels of stress that low LPC leaders have difficulty in coping with the situation; they find it difficult to know how much pressure to put onto followers and when to stand back and let things develop on their own.

The high LPC leader, on the other hand, prefers medium stress situations. In high stress situations, they tend to become overconcerned with the feelings of the followers, whilst in low stress situations they tend to worry about how they are coming across. This tends to result in their inventing tasks simply to prove their value as the leader rather than tasks based on needs or priorities.

Fiedler suggests that leaders should vary the stress level in a given situation to match their own preferred level as prescribed by the LPC and this is done by adjusting the relationship between the leader and the followers, by reinforcing position power and by modifying the extent to which tasks are structured and made clear with guidelines.

Fiedler's approach does have its critics, though it must be said that the LPC is a good predictor with regard to the optimum stress level for a given leader. The fact that the model provides three specific control variables to allow the leader to adjust the situation to match his or her own preference is a novel one. Once again, therefore, we return to process. It is the leader adjusting the stress level to provide the optimum *process* that he or she can handle that is the basis of Fiedler's work. One of the main criticisms of the Fiedler approach is that it suggests that the leader is either interested primarily in the task, or in the people, in a given situation while on an intuitive level we know that there are countless situations where the leader is interested in both aspects. Furthermore, LPC scores, like most psychological descriptions, are likely to be subject to a normal distribution throughout society. Thus most people will tend to be in the middle range, neither solely task-oriented nor solely relationship-oriented.

The task–relationship idea has merit, but it has to be seen as a mix of behaviours, not either/or. Two approaches which do acknowledge the mix are the Mouton–Blake grid and the Hersey–Blanchard life cycle approach.

The Mouton–Blake Grid

In the Mouton–Blake grid (Figure 2.6), devised in 1964 by two American researchers, five distinct styles of leadership are suggested, based on the mix of task and relationship behaviour. 9.1 style is very task-oriented, with little concern for the thoughts or feelings of the followers: 'Let's get the job done in spite of the followers' is a typical attitude of this type of leader. 1.9 is almost the opposite of this style. The leader values good relationships with the followers more highly than achieving task objectives: 'We all get on well around here, even if we don't produce much' is the typical attitude portrayed by this style.

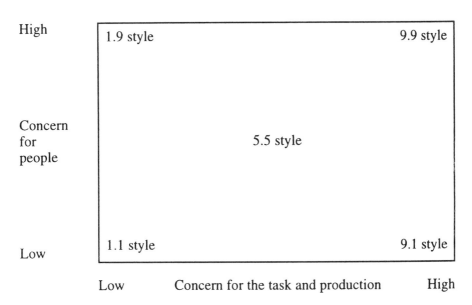

Figure 2.6   The Mouton–Blake grid

9.9 is the 'enthusiastic' leadership style which stresses a high level of task direction, interaction and encouragement as regards the followers. This is often the sign of an immature or newly promoted leader who feels that he or she must be seen to be acting as the leader all the time, regardless of the situation. 1.1 style is the 'hands off' or non-involvement leadership style. There are many situations where this can be an appropriate style. An increasing aspect of modern organizations is that leaders are often promoted to positions where their followers have more experience and technical knowledge than they have. In this situation, it is obviously inappropriate for a leader to be highly directive without taking into consideration the competence and experience levels of the followers. However, an alternative view of the 1.1 style of leadership is that it can be a sign of abdication, of the leader losing the will to perform effectively.

In the middle of the grid, we can identify the 5.5 style of leadership which is a balanced approach involving a moderate amount of behaviour in terms of both task/production and relationship/people aspects. One of the strong features of the 5.5 style is that it suggests that the leader can vary his or her style to be more or less task- or relationship-oriented as appropriate. In short, there is more scope for matching the style of the leader to the demands of the situation.

The Hersey–Blanchard Life Cycle Approach

Another approach to the issue of leadership style is that of Hersey and Blanchard (1969). This approach also suggests a number of leadership styles based on the mix of task and relationship behaviour. With this approach, however, there are four specific quadrants (see Figure 2.7) rather than the five styles suggested by Mouton and Blake. Furthermore, there is a progression based on the optimum style dependent on the ability of the followers to act as an integrated group. The suggestion is that a group of followers that has not worked together requires highly directive or task-oriented behaviour. This corresponds to a 'telling' type of leadership style and is referred to as quadrant 1 leadership style. In Mouton–Blake terms it is equivalent to 9.1 leadership style. The Mouton–Blake 9.9 style becomes quadrant 2 in the Hersey–Blanchard approach, with both high task and high relationship behaviour being displayed on the part of the leader, which corresponds to a 'selling' style. Moving to quadrant 3, we find the 'joining' approach, which involves the leader operating primarily through communication and encouragement, with little actual direction being given. Quadrant 4 is the 'delegating' or 'hands off' style, where leaders give little in the way of direction and only interact with the followers when necessary in terms of resources or crisis intervention. If we examine these four quadrants in terms of their styles, it is relatively easy to address the issue of 'group maturity'. An 'immature' group is one which has not bonded together to work as an effective team. This lack of cohesion may be due to the team being newly formed or it may be a result of individuals within the team working in isolation. In contrast, a 'mature' group is one which understands its objectives, possesses adequate levels of competence and can operate with minimal direction. It is, in effect, a self-led and self-managed team.

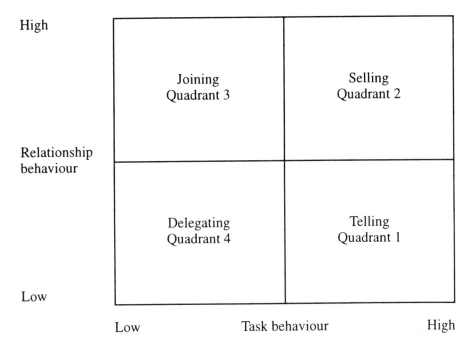

High

Relationship
behaviour

Low

Joining Quadrant 3	Selling Quadrant 2
Delegating Quadrant 4	Telling Quadrant 1

Low   Task behaviour   High

Figure 2.7   The Hersey–Blanchard life cycle approach

Hersey and Blanchard suggest that one of the main roles of a leader is to diagnose the level of maturity of the team of followers and then to operate in one of the four quadrants as appropriate. For an immature team, this will be quadrant 1; then, as team maturity develops, the suggestion is that the leader should progress from high task/low relationship behaviour by increasing the relationship aspect without reducing the direction. This will take him or her into quadrant 2. As the team matures even further, we can see that it will be appropriate to move from quadrant 2 to quadrant 3 and then to quadrant 4.

The converse is also true. If we take the situation of a 'mature' team whose performance has started to deteriorate, the Hersey–Blanchard approach will suggest that the leader should first operate in quadrant 4 by observing rather than intervening. If this fails to produce a performance improvement, quadrant 3 is appropriate, creating a dialogue with the team members to diagnose the problem areas. If this fails then actual direction as well as encouragement is appropriate (quadrant 2) with quadrant 1, strong direction, being the last resort. We should also notice that the concept of 'leadership distance' becomes relevant in terms of the Hersey–Blanchard approach. Quadrant 1 corresponds to the leader being apart from the group in terms of psychological distance. As the relationship aspect develops, this distance reduces progressively. In quadrant 4, the distance is actually controlled by the followers rather than the leader. If the followers have problems, they can approach the leader as necessary and this may involve relatively explicit and open communications. A 'mature group' needs little actual task or relationship behaviour from the leader. What they need, however, is to be able to use the leader as a resource when there are problems or when additional resources must be gained.

The Hersey–Blanchard approach boils down to the identification of the task and relationship dimensions and considering the application of various mixes of those behaviours to various situations. The problem is that all the task–relationship approaches are basically lacking in that they only consider part of the process, the part linked to specific behaviour. On an intuitive as well as a logic level, there has to be more to leadership than simply pure behaviour.

The Composite Approach to Leadership

Having explored a number of approaches to leadership and the process of development of the thought on the subject, we believe we are now at the 'composite stage' of leadership which recognizes that leadership is related more to a process than to an individual. It is, however, a process which is created and fuelled by an individual. In order to understand the process, it is important to acknowledge that part of understanding leadership involves understanding leadership models, recognizing that each model has a part to play. However, no single leadership model can ever be totally descriptive. It is important to use a mix of models, at least as a starting point. Understanding leadership also calls for observation of role models, evaluation and introspection on personal experience both as a leader and as a follower, together with sound conceptual research.

The aim of effective leadership has to be to transform performance by a group or an individual, to enable them to achieve objectives which they could not otherwise achieve. What, then, is this process that the individual creates? We argue that there is a linkage between leader attributes and action, leadership process and transformed individuals. The aspect of leader attributes and action involves a number of clearly observable elements. Of crucial importance is vision: effective leaders need to be able to create a mental picture of the future as they would wish it to be – the 'visioning process'. It is the transmission of this vision to the followers that plays such an important part in terms of emotional impact, a process of winning both hearts and minds. Another key issue is that the leader is in a position to act as a powerful role model. People tend to copy the behaviour they see, rather than doing what they are told, and so the leader can play an important part in shaping organizational behaviour by acting as he or she wants the followers to behave. Many ineffective leaders consistently say one thing and do another and this lack of congruence undermines the belief of the followers in the integrity of the leader. When behaviour matches rhetoric, you have an essential part of the transformational leadership process.

Transformation means that individual followers are induced to give enhanced performances which they would find difficult or impossible were it not for the actions of the leader. This effect is widely recognized and forms much of the basis for the current empowerment movement in organizations. There is also a recognition that the majority of individuals operate on only a small part of their potential abilities, so one of the approaches of effective, transformational leaders must be to unlock the potential abilities possessed by every follower.

Communication skills are vital in the way the leader operates, in particular to meet the challenges presented by two persistent cries: 'Nobody ever tells me what is going on!' and 'Nobody ever asks me my opinion!' Effective leaders must understand the importance of effective formal communication and of the tendencies of organizations to create and foster rumours. The efficient management of rumour control is an important part of leadership.

Change is another key aspect which our exploration of leadership theory must address as it is invariably the role of the leader to act as a change agent to bring about a new order of things. We have already referred to a number of differences between leadership and management. One of the most important differences is seen in the area of outcomes. This aspect has been identified by a number of researchers (see, in particular, Kotter, 1990) who suggest that a main function of management is to create predictable outcomes, whereas leadership seeks to promote change. This change involves movement towards the vision, at the same time acknowledging the existing situation and present trends if it is to be effective. The role of the leader as change agent is thus a vitally important one. Change is never comfortable; individuals resist change because it challenges their 'comfort zones' and can present them with fear of the unknown. Leaders who help individuals cope with change and then develop an ability to seek and promote change are what we need for the future.

Returning to leadership theory, the Hersey–Blanchard approach in particular would suggest that one of the main goals of a leader should be to make themselves redundant in operational terms on a daily basis. The followers should be so competent and confident that the day-to-day situations can be managed by them without the direct involvement of the leader. This involves adapting to change and then actively seeking opportunities to improve things. This frees the leader from the routine operational issues and enables him or her to pay attention to the more strategic issues, including that of vision. However, the leader does still have an important role in operational terms, although it should be an infrequent one: it is during crisis that the leader comes into his or her own.

These areas of leader attributes and action combine to create what we call the basis for leadership competence, which we will explore further in Chapter 7. The working model of leadership which we have developed represents the state of the art in terms of thought on leadership as a process, and may be used in the real world as an operational guide. The key to understanding our model is to look at leadership as a transformational process, created by effective action stemming from an individual. That is, it is a process which enables individuals and teams to achieve objectives which they would otherwise find impossible. This transformational aspect leads us to consider the four fundamental aspects of the leadership process: vision, values, communication and behaviour. The full leadership process is shown in Figure 2.8.

Let us summarize what the model in Figure 2.8 is proposing. Leaders set direction by having a vision or a goal, but it is important that the vision is not taken in isolation. Those visions that become reality are invariably 'tuned in' to trends, so a major part of effective visioning skills has to be the idea of becoming aware of what is happening in the environment in which a leader is operating. We have already mentioned the flexibility/consistency issue: how can a leader be flexible and consistent at the same time? We believe the answer is provided by the issue of values. Values provide a sense of direction, even in the most difficult circumstances, and awareness of their importance is one of the prime functions of the leader.

The communication role of the leader is also important, in terms of communicating both the vision and the values. As followers believe what they see rather than what they are told, leader communication involves behaviour as well as the spoken word and the impact that the leader makes as a role model must never be overlooked.

These four key elements combine to create the ambient culture in which the leader operates. It is the culture, be it constructive, aggressive or defensive, which will determine to a large extent the success of the leader in terms of promoting change in the followers' behaviour. Initiatives in organizations, such as total quality, empowerment and customer orientation are more dependent on the operational culture of the organization than is perhaps generally realized. In addition, when problems arise, it is the way the problems are resolved and whether that resolution takes place with reference to the value set that is important.

The basis of the leadership process thus involves both leader attributes and actions creating a process which transforms the followers so that they

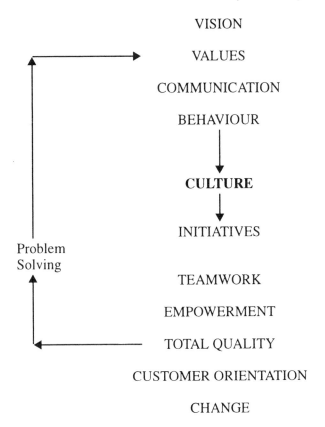

Figure 2.8   The leadership process

develop the ability to achieve more than they would if the leader had not been involved.

Summary

In this chapter we have considered the development of leadership theory. We have considered the attempts at defining leadership, together with some ideas on levels and style of leadership. We have also considered the thought process, moving from the qualities approach, through the situational approach to both the functional and behavioural approaches. Having explored the development of leadership in this way, we have concluded that there is no single leadership approach which explains the phenomenon fully. What is needed is a composite approach which takes into account a range of models, personal experience, role models, introspection and case study research.

Our thesis revolves around the idea that the role of the individual leader must not be undervalued. This is not, however, a reversion to the qualities approach. We believe that effective leaders, through the combination of certain actions and competencies, create a leadership process which serves to transform their followers. In so doing, they inspire their followers to perform considerably better than their normal levels of performance. This idea will be explored further, later on in the book, but first we need to look at what is happening today and, in particular, the way effective leadership can add value to the organization. Many organizations are encountering difficulties in a world increasingly subject to change and it is often the case that those responsible for leadership find the task daunting. The impact of this accelerating rate of change on individuals means that our leaders will have to be more effective than ever before in creating an environment within the organization where individuals actively embrace change.

References

Adair, J. (1983), *Effective Leadership*, London: Pan.

Blake, R.R. and Mouton, J.S. (1964), *The Managerial Grid*, Houston: Gulf Publishing.

Fiedler, F.E., Chemers, M. and Mahar, L. (1976), *Improving Leadership Effectiveness: The Leader Match Concept*. New York: Wiley.

Forgas, J. (1979), *Social Episodes*, European Association of Experimental Social Psychology, in association with Academic Press.

Hamel, G. and Prahalad, C.K. (1994), *Competing for the Future*, Boston: Harvard Business School Press.

Hersey, P. and Blanchard, K.H. (1969), *Management of Organization Behavior*, Englewood Cliffs, NJ: Prentice-Hall.

Kotter, J.P. (1990), *A Force for Change*, New York: The Free Press.

Stogdill, R.M. (1974), *Handbook of Leadership: a survey of theory and research*, London, Macmillan.

3   How Effective Leadership Adds Value

Why Do We Need Leaders at All?

In this chapter we are going to consider three issues. First, there is the issue of what leaders actually contribute to our organizations; that is, what value do they add? Second, we are going to suggest why many of our organizations are finding life difficult, partly as the result of leadership issues. Third, we will look at the subject of change and how the leader can contribute to the effective adaptation of the organization to the changes in its environment.

What Do We Mean by Added Value?

For many years now, many organizations in the West have focused on status and the level of the organization in which the individual finds himself. However, the situation is changing and, rather than relying on status, the leader of the future must be adding value, which leads to the main question posed by this chapter: just how is it that leaders can add value? If this cannot be answered, then the role of leader is, in itself, dubious. Leaders in the future as well as in the present will come under much closer scrutiny than ever before in terms of the value that they add to their organizations.

Figure 3.1 gives a useful insight into what, in organizational terms, we mean by added value. The concept relates to the idea that each individual, in this case the leader, is presented with a situation or task as their input work. The leader then operates in such a way as to 'make things better'; that is, the output is more valuable than the input. Take, for example, a typical basic leadership episode of a group of people needing to cross a river with some planks, rope and an oil drum. In this case, the leader is presented with resources (namely the people and the materials) and then he or she creates a plan and briefs the group in order to marshal the resources and bind the

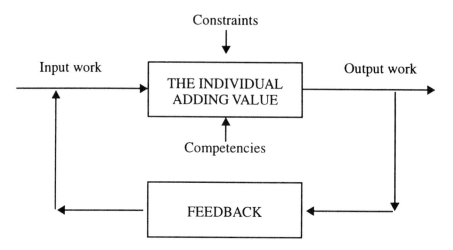

Figure 3.1   The concept of added value

group together to work on the common objective of crossing the river. In this example, the leader adds value by coordinating the efforts of all concerned and helping them to achieve the objective.

It is important to notice that leadership is not a one-way open loop system. Effective leaders gain feedback about the value that they are adding and adjust their operation accordingly. If we consider the role of the leader or manager in the organization, this relates very closely to the appraisal process which is basically a feedback mechanism to help individuals at all levels in the organization add more value. In addition, it is important to realize that any individual is always subject to constraints in terms of their ability to add value. This may be due to a lack of external physical resources, perhaps because of financial constraints, or it may be due to internal challenges such as negative beliefs, a lack of motivation or excessive fear of punishment if attempts to innovate are not successful.

Finally, in the added value model, we have the idea of competencies. In this context we are using the word 'competencies' to refer to those behaviours and attributes which an individual needs to possess or be capable of harnessing in order to maximize the contribution they can make to the organization. We will discuss specific leadership competencies in Chapter 7.

It is this mixture of factors which is now reshaping the concept of the individual in the organization. Effective leaders of the future need to concentrate on how to enable their followers to add maximum value rather than simply occupy a role and blindly follow the rules of the organization. There are many ways in which a leader can make a difference. First, it seems that effective leaders manage the emotional energy of their respective organizations. Many writers have referred to the concept of transformational leadership, as we have done in Chapter 2. This involves getting the best out of people, harnessing their emotional energy in the service of the organizational mission to pursue its vision and its goals. Second, effective leaders are intimately involved in the issue of change, ensuring that the organization adapts to its changing environment and that it stays ahead of the competition in the business world. Third, and perhaps most important, effective leaders have the responsibility of creating an effective organizational culture, one in which individuals are triggered to tap into their potential at the individual level while helping the organization to achieve its objectives and making the corporate vision reality.

Among the many definitions of organizational culture is one which suggests that it is 'the way things happen around here'. This is an interesting definition and one which has been developed commercially. One organizational culture inventory (OCI) marketed by Verax Limited looks at organizational culture on three basic dimensions, each of which contains four behavioural patterns related to a positive or negative aspect of the way organizations operate. The first of the three dimensions relates to the constructive behaviours linked to setting goals, developing people, creating a helpful, humanistic culture where problems can be openly discussed and where good cross-functional team operation exists. These are all beneficial in creating a healthy culture. The second area involves defensive behaviours related to the excessive need for approval, overreliance on convention and dependence on higher authority, together with risk aversion, tend to minimize the contribution which the individual can make. These behaviours characterize the organization where a 'fear culture' exists, where the individual is loath to innovate in case things go wrong and he or she receives punishment.

The third area relates to internal aggression. We have already mentioned the idea of the leader managing the emotional energy of the organization and, as will be seen later, this becomes significant when we consider the third area of this approach to organizational culture, namely the degree to which internal aggression tends to exist within the organization. This is highlighted by the extent to which four distinct behavioural patterns present themselves. The first of these is where individuals devote considerable time and energy to building their own power bases – what we might call empire building. This is a sign of insecurity and one which tends to be counterproductive with regard to the operation of the organization as a whole. The second pattern is that of perfectionism where there is a constant striving for a 'zero mistakes' situation and where mistakes are punished rather than being seen as a source of learning. Although the ideas of 'total quality' of 'right first time' and 'zero defect' are laudable, if taken too far they can lead to a culture characterized by attribution of blame, rather than healthy innovation. The third behavioural pattern is concerned with oppositional behaviour where new ideas are always opposed, regardless of their merit. This tends to fuel the 'us and them' aspect of organizational life in terms of cross-functional relationships. Finally, we have internal competitiveness where different functions within the organization devote their energy more to fighting each other than to working towards the benefit of the organization as a whole.

All these ideas can be expressed in terms of the management of the internal energy of the organization. Peter Senge, in his landmark book *The Fifth Discipline*, created a very elegant model to display graphically the process of internal energy management, or 'alignment' as he called it, in relation to the sort of teamwork displayed in a sports team, in this case the Boston Celtics basketball team. Chapter 7 develops the concept of alignment as the management of human energy in terms of its being a prime leadership competence. At this stage, however, we focus on the energy aspect. There is a simple mathematical approach which gives a useful insight into the importance of managing human energy within the organization to avoid the pitfall of cross-functional difficulties. Figure 3.2 shows the basic idea.

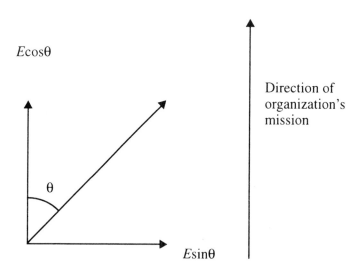

Note: E = energy of 'non-aligned' individual; $E\cos\theta$ = component of energy in line with organizational mission; $E\sin\theta$ = component of energy at right angles to organizational mission.

Figure 3.2   The concept of alignment

Consider the general case of an individual with an energy level E contributing to the work of the organization. We can see that, with a non-aligned individual, some of his or her energy is in parallel with the organizational mission (shown as $E\cos\theta$), being less than the potential energy the individual could be contributing. What is of some concern is that some of the individual's energy is at right angles to the organizational mission (shown up as $E\sin\theta$). This is the energy component which tends to oscillate across the organization, resulting in the aggressive type of behaviour discussed earlier which tends to lead to destructive organizational politics. The leader's main role in energy management is to minimize the $E\sin\theta$ component and maximize the $E\cos\theta$ component.

The Old Organization

Human beings have a tendency to dwell on the positive aspects of the past. However, in terms of how organizations operate, this may not now be as appropriate as we might think. Many organizations were highly autocratic, very rigid, producer-centred and operated in the market-place in a 'win or lose' type of approach. Command, control and predictability were the order of the day and the resulting operational systems tended to create status conscious hierarchies. The significance of the individual was characterized more by the size of the office they occupied and the company car they drove than by the degree to which they contributed in real terms to the functioning of the organization. Communications tended to be top-down only and resulted in people doing what was expected of them and no more. In many respects the boss–worker relationship was akin to that of a parent and child, with the assumption being made that the boss knew all the answers and the individual workers simply had to obey orders. We revisit this idea in Chapter 5, when we recall the highly perceptive observation of Matsuchita about the difference between the general approaches of Western and Eastern management styles in terms of tapping into the ability of the workforce to make suggestions and solve problems effectively.

These characteristics are reminiscent of a paternalism where people know their place, work within an accepted framework, work to please their boss and never consider challenging the status quo. In the best case it is benign, in the worst case it can lead to a 'fear culture'. Furthermore, the 'jobs for life' idea is not the route to corporate excellence if we really want to tap into the energy of the workforce.

In many of our more conventional organizations, there is a distinct lack of awareness of what life is actually like on the front line in terms of the fear culture. If the bottom line is acceptable in financial terms, if profits are rising, then senior management can be misled into thinking all is well throughout the organization. Even if they ask the people at the sharp end of the operation how things are going, they only tend to be told the things they want to hear rather than a true account of how things are in terms of morale on the front line.

This situation has now changed for many of our forward-looking organizations and will have to be taken into account by the rest if they are to survive, let alone develop. This transition from the old hierarchy to new ways of working is causing difficulty for many organizations. As a result, insecurity is growing in the perceptions of many of the workforce and this is leading to the development of fear cultures in many instances because individuals are frightened to take the risk of innovation in case things go wrong and they lose their jobs. We label this challenge the 'safety first' approach and it does much to limit the innovative activity of many organizations.

Where Are We Now?

Organizations are under considerable pressure to adapt to the environments in which they now find themselves. The well-known management guru Tom Peters once stated that 'predictability is a thing of the past' and this, in a nutshell, is the major challenge that organizations are now facing. The future is not going to be like the past in terms of stability, predictability and clear-cut 'black and white' solutions to problems. We have to realize that the future will require flexibility, adaptability and speed of response, and the pursuit of a clearly defined mission with consistent values. For many organizations, this is a difficult task, particularly if they are very bureaucratic in their style of operation.

The Accelerating Rate of Change

Most writers and commentators seem to agree that the rate of change that we are currently experiencing is the most rapid yet encountered by the human race. In particular, the advances in technology mean that fundamental changes are taking place in society at all levels and in almost all areas of the world. The 'Information Superhighway' means that we have the potential to communicate with each other worldwide as never before, but it is important to realize that technology should be the servant of the human race and not its master. Thus leaders need to embrace the new technologies and integrate them into their leadership operation more than ever before.

Our Attitude to Change: the Human Paradox

Although the human being is a very adaptable organism in terms of ability to create and operate in new environments, the ability of individuals to cope with both of these aspects of change varies widely. A pedestrian rate of change for one individual can be threatening for another and, consequently, one of the prime roles of the leader in the modern organization is to develop the abilities of all followers within the organization to enable them to thrive on the change process.

There is an apparent paradox here. The fact that human beings become bored surprisingly quickly, and that many need the stimulation of change, has been demonstrated conclusively by experiments on sensory deprivation and solitary confinement. This being so, it is natural to think that individuals would not only enjoy change but actively seek it. In reality, of course, it is the areas of change and the extent of change within those areas that are important; and some people need stability in their lives to perform at their best. In simple terms, we seek both change and stability at the same time.

A Cascade of Change

People have been exposed to an enormous amount of change during the past 20 years or so: global changes, changes in the business environment and organizational changes. Global changes are not too difficult to cope with if the individual is not personally involved, but, as reported by the media, they lead to a perception that the world is becoming a less desirable place to live, and perhaps the main consequence of this exposure is that individuals become increasingly aware of their personal safety and security needs. In a way, this is a reversal of what we might think the natural process of the development of civilization, with a greater emphasis on higher-order needs than on basic and safety needs. It is interesting at this stage to recall the work of Abraham Maslow who, in the 1960s, suggested that human beings display a hierarchy of needs (Figure 3.3).

At the most basic level, individuals have needs such as air, food and water in order to survive. Once these needs are more or less satisfied, attention moves towards satisfying safety and security needs. Moving up the hierarchy, the individual then needs to satisfy social belonging needs, then needs relating to ego and self-esteem and, finally, self-actualization needs. It is this last area of need that is perhaps most crucial in terms of the role of the leader in the future. If we are truly to tap into the realms of human potential, there must be a shift towards addressing self-actualization needs and away from basic and safety needs. This will undoubtedly become a major issue for leadership in the future.

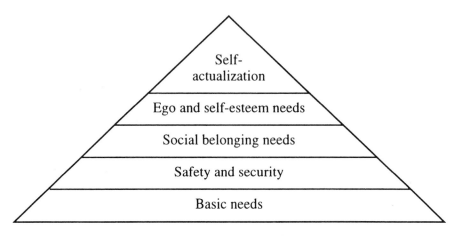

Figure 3.3   Maslow's hierarchy of needs

It is therefore important to understand what these self-actualization needs are and why they are important. To understand this fully, we need to consider how the human race has progressed over the centuries. There seems to be little doubt that, in its early stages, the human race was basically cave-dwelling, killing for survival, operating at the lowest of Maslow's levels of needs. Then, as the human race started to exercise more control over its environment, there was a shift towards an Agricultural Age, with the support systems of blacksmiths, traders and so forth. Next came the Industrial Age of the late 1800s, and the Capital Age of the early and mid-1900s. What we have seen in the latter half of the twentieth century is the development of the Information Age, in which we are firmly involved at the present time. Many have claimed that the next age will be the 'Leisure Age', although this was predicted as far back as the late 1970s. While it is true that there is a significant number of unemployed in most of the countries of the Western world, those individuals who are in work seem to be working harder and for longer hours than ever before. This is evidenced by the cost of stress in the workplace that seems to be an increasing phenomenon. In the United Kingdom alone, stress has been estimated as costing around 100 million working days each year. Based on an approximate workforce of around 17 million individuals, this amounts, on average, to six days lost per individual per year – hardly indicative of a society which is becoming more leisure-based in its orientation.

There is a straightforward answer to this quandary. Those people who are in work, particularly in organizations, are being placed under increasing pressure to add value. The processes of downsizing and restructuring both tend to result in reduced headcount whilst at the same time seeking increased productivity.

Where Are We Heading?

While those who are in work do not have the time for more leisure, those who have the time for more leisure pursuits do not have the money. As a result, the Leisure Age seems an unlikely destination for the human race as a whole. We believe that the future is indicated by Maslow's approach and that the next identifiable age will be that of the realization of human potential. The signs are already there, as illustrated by the evidence that, for the past decade, there has been a growth worldwide of the human potential movement. In the United States, the neurolinguistic programming (NLP) movement initiated by John Grinder and Richard Bandler has become a powerful influence in the world of training. In basic terms, NLP could be described as the technology of human excellence and it started with the originators carrying out a number of studies of various individuals who had become world leaders in their particular fields. It may thus be the initial thrust of what could be the next stage in the development of the human race, the age of understanding how to tap into the potential abilities that all human beings possess. We will investigate the potential offered by NLP to the leadership process in the next chapter.

The changes in the business environment over the past two decades have been very significant, but, while these are of interest, they tend not to affect too seriously the individual unless their personal livelihood is threatened. The resultant organizational changes may be coped with fairly successfully if an individual has stability in the other areas of her or his life. The challenge we are now facing is that all three of the levels mentioned earlier are becoming volatile at the same time: global, business and organizational changes are combining to make the present time potentially less stable than almost any other period in history. During the past ten years, we have seen fundamental shifts in world politics as well as in the business world. The East–West divide has faded away to provide opportunities for a tremendous expansion in the world market-place particularly in terms of countries that have been outside the market economies for many years. Competition on a global basis is a real issue for many businesses and has caused them to re-examine their operations.

In an increasing number of organizations, the shift towards customer orientation and quality of service has been notable, in word if not always in deed. However, this shift is only part of the story. We have identified seven primary organizational process changes apparent in the public and private sectors, and in both manufacturing and service areas.

First, organizations are reducing their levels of management by 'delayering' (reducing layers in the management hierarchy) and downsizing (reducing resource usage, including headcount, to produce the same or greater output). The result of this is that the leaders at the top of the organization will have to develop the ability of everyone within the organization to compensate for those levels of management that will no longer exist. Second, people are looking more towards 'portfolio' working lives than ever before: increasingly, they are looking for ways to spread the risk of their financial ruin by having more than one job. The organization of the future may well find itself having to compete for high-quality labour, rather than being oversubscribed, as many appear to be present; leaders will need to sell their organizations as a good place to be.

The third identifiable area of change relates to job security. It is no longer possible to guarantee any individual a job for life because nobody knows what the future holds in any industry for more than a few months ahead. No job is secure and people need to become more flexible to cope with changes in the basic nature of their working life, even if they stay in the one organization. This will require everyone to have greater self-knowledge and to be a leader in their own right and at their appropriate level in terms of their ability to show initiative in an increasingly complex and uncertain world.

The fourth area relates to maintaining the competitive edge. To remain competitive, the organization needs to operate with increasing speed and responsiveness. This means that front-line employees need to be empowered with more decision-making responsibility, rather than relying on permission from their manager or leader.

The fifth change reflects the development of the human race. The progression of our society through the agricultural, industrial and information ages leads us to consider what will be the next stage. As we have already said, many leading thinkers are predicting that the next era will be that of tapping into the creative resources of the human mind much more effectively than we have done to date. Leaders will have to understand that people are capable of achieving tremendous results if they are allowed to develop to their fullest potential. This is the point to which we have already referred in terms of Maslow's concept of 'self-actualization'.

Sixth is the shift that is taking place with regard to the basic role of the manager, from authoritarian boss to a sort of coach. Virtually every client with whom we have come into contact recently is redefining the role of the manager to take account of this shift and trying to work out, in operational day-to-day terms, how to use the human resource more effectively. In doing so, they are attempting to trigger the process of tapping into the potential abilities of the workforce by developing individuals to meet future challenges, rather than simply training them for the present.

Last on our list is the concept of the 'Virtual Organization'. With the explosion in the use of information technology comes the exciting possibility that people do not have to operate from the same geographical site but may be spread over hundreds or even thousands of miles. We see this happening with a number of organizations who are using increasing numbers of temporary staff and also consultants for fixed-term projects, rather than incurring a large cost base with fixed overheads of salaries and wages. In its ultimate form, the Virtual Organization is one that exists only on paper, with a tiny physical hub. Instead of a large office and production staff, it relies on a network of individuals connected by telephone, fax and computer modems, which produces environmental benefits in that people will reduce their need to travel to work. It may well be that, for many workers, physical travel is almost completely displaced by electronic travel and this could have many benefits, including less stress, less environmental damage and less time wasted. Individuals will be able to use their time more effectively if they spend it on productive work rather than travelling. The Virtual Organization, however, produces the problem of isolation: the human being is a social animal which needs the stimulation of others to perform well, so the effective leader of the future will have to develop skills to unite people and enable them to feel part of a team even if they are widespread in geographical terms.

In the context of these changes, what of the idea of 'managing change?' In fact, there is a real concern about this concept because the very word 'managing' implies control and predictable outcomes, and this is not the essence of what our organizations need. There are many more suitable words than managing – enabling, facilitating, initiating, adapting, promoting and coordinating, to name a few. The reason for this is the need to alter the perception of the management population towards leadership concepts rather than those relating to pure management. This is the essence of 'leadership for change'; we have already learnt from Kotter that management is to do with control and predictability. Leadership, as we have already said, involves setting direction, emotion and people's feelings. These are aspects which have not yet been fully realized by the business community of the West.

Change is Here to Stay

Change is here to stay. It is unlikely that, in the foreseeable future, organizations will return to the relative stability of the middle of the twentieth century, which means that leaders at all levels will require enhanced skills, particularly in terms of helping the followers cope with, and actually thrive on, change. This ought not to be impossible, but we need to shift the perception of change from threat to opportunity and leaders at all levels will need significant enhancement of their ability to help produce this movement on the part of their followers. There are a number of issues involved in skilful 'uncertainty leadership and management'.

First, we have to understand that, although individuals do have tremendous internal resources to cope with change, there is only a certain amount of change which can be accommodated at any one time. The research work of Holmes and Rahe in the 1960s on the impact on health of significant life changes gives considerable support for this argument. In their research, the medical histories of a large number of individuals were correlated with the amount of change that they had experienced in their lives and each significant change, or 'life event' as Holmes and Rahe termed them, had a relative score attached to it. Top of the list, with 100 points, was the death of a spouse, while less traumatic events such as job changes, holidays and so on were awarded fewer 'change points'. What emerged from this study was that each of us can handle change up to a certain level. However, once that level is exceeded, health problems can ensue. To a certain extent, the role of the leader needs to include the skill of helping individuals to cope with developing their ability to cope with change.

In order to adapt to change, individuals need to pass through four stages and it is a basic maxim of leadership for change that the leader understands how to facilitate these changes and promote the individual's development through them. The phases of change reaction that individuals pass through seem to be as follows: (1) denial – refusing to acknowledge the change as valid or necessary; (2) resistance – actively opposing the change; (3) exploration – exploring various aspects of the change; and (4) commitment – developing the realization that the change is beneficial. These phases are plotted in two dimensional-form in Figure 3.4. In the initial stages of a change, individuals often refuse to admit that it is necessary, seeing it as outside their sphere of influence, control or even interest. To a certain extent, they believe that, if the problem is ignored, it will go away. This is what we mean by the 'externalization' of the change. As things progress, however, individuals often see the change as an increasing threat and tend to internalize its impact. The threat level increases and the individual takes active steps to resist the change. This may take the form of participating to a small extent and then, unconsciously perhaps, sabotaging the change by proving that new procedures and so forth do not work. This can be a subconscious rather than a conscious process because people do not normally set out consciously to prove that the change is for the worse – it is their subconscious or unconscious mind which takes the lead.

EXTERNALIZATION OF CHANGE

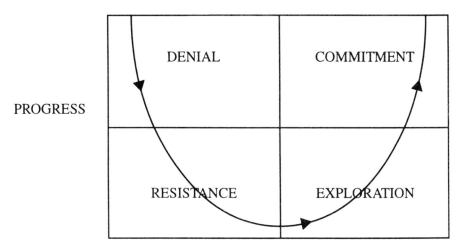

INTERNALIZATION OF CHANGE

Figure 3.4   Individual reaction phases to the process of change

The art of leading through change is to counter the tendency of this apparent sabotage effect by giving the individual small steps of success in terms of outcomes. It relies on the individual concentrating on the positive benefits of embracing the change and finding that it works better than the 'old way'. Rather than change being seen as a punishment or a liability, it should be seen as a positive benefit. It is the role of the leader to ensure that the small success steps are created properly and that the individual is automatically led towards the fourth stage of commitment. Coping with change on the individual level is largely a matter of managing the individual's self-esteem. If the person feels good about himself, his ability to cope with change will be greatly enhanced; if his self-esteem suffers, for whatever reason, his ability to cope will be greatly reduced.

Perhaps the fundamental thing for leaders to bear in mind during times of change is the paradox referred to earlier: human beings seek change and stimulation, but not too much at the same time. The art of leadership during times of change may well be as much to do with creating stability zones as with areas for change and development.

The Role of the Leader in Managing Uncertainty

We believe that, to lead effectively during times of uncertainty, leaders need to pay attention to a number of issues:

1   There needs to be a sound awareness of the present.
2   There needs to be a sound awareness of trends for the future.
3   Resources need to be managed effectively. Effective leaders have never restricted themselves purely to physical resources; levels of aspiration, of inspiration, of motivation and morale are also resources and in some ways they are even more important than material issues. Effective leaders for the future will pay just as much attention to these issues as managers of the past have paid to the hard issues of finance and so forth.
4   Inspiration and alignment are fundamental to the effective management of organizational energy.
5   The way towards the vision is just as vital as the vision itself. It is no good simply having a wonderful picture of the future if there are no specific plans to make that vision reality.

We believe that we are now in a position to identify some specific leadership competencies which we will explore in Chapter 7. However, for the purposes of the present chapter, we need to revisit our basic model first. Leadership involves both leader attributes and leader action. This creates a leadership process which, instead of focusing on a given individual, turns its attention to the followers, the situation and the outcomes. For this to happen in times of uncertainty, leaders need to pay attention to a number of issues.

Leaders need to set a direction and mobilize the followers on an emotional level as well as an intellectual level to pursue a vision. Even if the vision in the short term is not the one achieved in the ultimate outcome, the fact that the followers are given a sense of purpose is in itself a useful mechanism for creating effective behaviour. It is vital, however, that the issue of predictability be addressed. Followers need to understand that the direction currently being followed may not in reality lead to the ultimate outcome and that the situation may change. In the past, when leaders have steadfastly locked onto a vision regardless of the changing situation, there have been some tragic outcomes. Norman Dixon (1976) quotes countless examples from military history that show the severe penalties to be paid by leaders and their followers who fail to adapt to a changing situation.

What is needed to cope with the present rate of change is a vision, an implementation programme and effective feedback which take into account both the current performance and the changing situation. As Tony Robbins, an NLP trainer, has suggested (1988), there does seem to be a four-part 'ultimate success formula' when it comes to human behaviour: decide what you want to achieve, take action, observe the results and change your behaviour appropriately if it is not producing the desired outcome. In the past we have seen leaders pay attention to the first two elements. In the future, it may well be the third and fourth factors which are the most important.

Leaders in the future will need to act more as role models than has been the case in the past and so bond themselves more firmly to their followers. John Adair (1989) has given us much food for thought in terms of the effective leader acting as a role model and example. Effective leaders in times of change seem to have the ability to mobilize their followers and to get the best out of them, which is the very essence of transformational leadership discussed above. In times of change, morale and self-esteem are key issues. The almost magical ability of some individuals to bring out the best in people despite all odds is a prime means of helping people cope with uncertainty.

A Tool for Value Added Change Leadership

To add value to an organization, the leader needs to understand the present situation, create a vision for an alternative future and then create a process for producing the required transition. One very useful approach is 'force field analysis', which is based on a graphical approach, as shown in Figure 3.5. Force field analysis is based on the idea that we can consider a present situation in relation to some alternative which is required in the future in terms of forces which are pushing the present situation towards the desired future situation. These forces are called 'driving forces'. At the same time, the future situation does not come about automatically because of factors which are maintaining the present situation and thus blocking progress. These forces are called 'restraining forces'. To apply force field analysis, the first stage is to identify the characteristics of the present situation and the desired characteristics of the future situation. Once this is achieved, it is necessary to identify the natural driving forces which are tending to push the present situation towards the desired situation. For example, if an organization wants to produce more widgets per hour, one of the driving forces may well be paying the workforce more money. At the same time, we have to acknowledge that there are invariably restraining forces – in this example, output to a given quality standard may be limited unless an investment is made in new equipment.

Once a full analysis is made of the present situation with regard to the driving forces and restraining forces, the leader can consider which of the

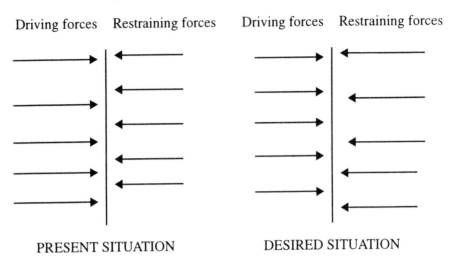

Figure 3.5   Force field analysis

forces may be addressed in order to create change. Where most organizations tend to go wrong is in trying to shift from the present to the future situation by simply stepping up the driving forces. Because people get locked into comfort zones, this increase in the driving forces frequently results in more resistance from the restraining forces, manifested by a 'resistance to change'. What happens is that the individuals concerned are placed under more pressure, which can lead to the stress problems which have already been mentioned.

What the leader needs to do is to concentrate on removing one or more of the restraining forces so that the natural balance of the status quo is altered. This allows the driving forces to move the situation towards the desired one in a natural way. It is at this stage that an increase in the driving forces is appropriate to speed up the transition which is already under way. Eventually, the system will settle down again into a new balance of driving forces and restraining forces and into the new situation. Change made in this way tends to gain much more commitment from all the participants than the more orthodox method of pushing hard against resistance.

Summary

In this chapter we have considered how leaders can add value in such a way as to create a healthy organizational culture. The rate of change within organizations is quickening dramatically and it is a prime role of the leader to become a 'change agent', developing ways to overcome the blockages and the resistance to change often generated by individuals. Many people see change as a threat and something to be avoided, yet we all live with change and many of us actively seek change in our lives outside work. The challenge for the leader is to exploit this and get individuals to be as flexible and adaptive in the working situation as they are in their domestic lives. Change and stress are often linked and effective change leadership can do much to reduce the cost of unnecessary stress in the workplace. Much of leadership is concerned with managing the transition from the present state to some desired future state and this involves the skill of defining and creating, mentally at first, that future state. The next chapter addresses this issue by dealing with the skills of foresight and vision, vital matters for the effective leader to consider.

References

Adair, J. (1989), *Great Leaders*, Guildford: Talbot Adair Press.

Dixon, N.F. (1976), *On the Psychology of Military Incompetence*, London: Jonathan Cape.

Holmes, T.H. and Rahe, R.H. (1967), 'The Social Readjustment Rating Scale', *Journal of Psychosomatic Research*, **2**, (2).

Robbins, A. (1988), *Unlimited Power*, London: Simon & Schuster.

Robbins, A. (1992), *Awaken the Giant Within*, London: Simon & Schuster.

Senge, P.M. (1993), *The Fifth Discipline*, London: Century Business.

Senge, P.M., Kleiner, Al, Roberts, C., Ross, R.B. and Smith, B.J. (1994), *The Fifth Discipline Fieldbook*, London: Nicholas Brealey Publishing Limited.

4   The Skills of Foresight and Vision

The Importance of Vision

Virtually every leadership model talks about the importance of the leader, at whatever level, being able to set a clear direction. Whether we talk in terms of defining the task, setting goals or inspiring people to take action towards a new future, the notion of the leader having some vision of the future state is an important one.

Visions on their own can be the basis for significant problems. The history books contain countless examples of individuals who have become obsessed with a personal vision of the future which is divorced from the current direction in which progress is being made. Whilst this can be beneficial in some circumstances to some individuals, for example with regard to Nelson Mandela's efforts to abolish apartheid in South Africa, it can lead to considerable upheaval in society. A vision should not just be an isolated personal interpretation of the future; it should be based on sound situational considerations and an awareness of trends in terms of where the current situation is heading. Thus, when we talk about vision, we prefer to use the amplified version of 'foresight and vision'. In many respects, our view of the visioning process is more akin to vehicle headlights reaching out into the darkness to create a visual pathway towards the destination.

There is a paradox in the leadership literature about the visioning process. As has already been stated, the process of setting future direction is frequently quoted as one of the prime functions and contributions of the effective leader. The paradox is that relatively little material has been written on how to actually carry out the visioning process. What does an individual actually *do* in terms of practical behaviours and actions to create a compelling vision of the future? To answer this question, we need to return briefly to the basics of what leaders actually contribute. Effective leaders, as we have already said, operate by creating a synergy between personal, situational and behavioural factors. In essence they have the mental skills to create a compelling vision, a sound awareness of the present situation, together with trend lines, and the practical ability to carry out certain actions which will lead to the vision becoming reality. It is this mix of leadership attributes rather than personality qualities which holds the key to effective leadership in the future.

Visionary leadership implies that the leader is able to develop a long-range vision of what his or her organization should become, while at the same time being able to create a pathway of medium and short-term milestones along the way. This vision and its elements need to be communicated in such a way that people want to 'buy into' it and help translate the vision into reality. Communication is obviously a key element in the visioning process. The vision must be expressed in such a way that it becomes an integral part of day-to-day life in the organization.

One American researcher, Marshall Sashkin (1986), identified a number of core thinking skills in terms of the visioning process and the most significant of these relates to expressing the vision and behaving in a way that advances the process of translation into reality. He proposes five key elements to do this:

1   creating a set of policy actions to involve everyone in the organization;
2   communicating with people at all levels in the organization to develop the details of the new policy;
3   regular communication sessions to work with managers and other employees to review progress;
4   working with managers at all levels to identify ways to track the effectiveness of the programme;
5   overseeing the monitoring of the programme and developing modifications as needed.

This is very much an operational approach in terms of practical action. There are, however, other skills which Sashkin has identified. The vision needs to be explained to others to ensure consistency of behaviour at all levels. The vision needs to be extended to all parts of the organization to ensure that everyone becomes emotionally involved. It needs to be expanded and to be all-embracing. Such action might include partnerships with customers such as that formed in the United Kingdom between The Body Shop and Peter Lane Transport which we outline below as a case study.

In order to understand how leaders may develop their ability at the visioning process, we need to consider some basic psychology and, indeed, the neurology of the human brain. In the 1960s, Roger Sperry of the University of

Case study. Peter Lane Transport and The Body Shop: A visionary case study on business partnership

Many businesses still operate in an adversarial way in terms of the relationship with their customers. In contrast to this established modus operandi, the case of Peter Lane Transport and The Body Shop outlined in a recent BBC business documentary is outstanding.

Peter Lane Transport is a transport and distribution company of some 300 plus employees based in Bristol, England. A fleet of over 200 vehicles is maintained to service the customer base. The company has become completely intertwined with one of its key customers, The Body Shop. The basis of the relationship is that Peter Lane Transport invested considerable time getting to know The Body Shop and identifying its specific needs as a customer. A joint vision of service level was created in terms of the standards of performance required of Peter Lane Transport to deliver to each of Body Shop's 233 retail outlets.

Regular meetings are held and Peter Lane Transport personnel are actually based in the customer's own warehouse in Littlehampton, Sussex, rather than in their own premises in Bristol. The service level agreement of 99.7 per cent of all deliveries being in a specified two-hour 'window' results in Peter Lane Transport receiving a bonus if they exceed the required standard. At the time of writing, they were receiving maximum bonus, providing a service level in excess of 99.9 per cent.

The key to creating such outstanding service is the attitude of the front-line workforce. Every individual in the Peter Lane Group reflects an attitude of total job ownership in psychological terms and feels valued in terms of their contribution. They are all aware of the corporate vision and work on a daily basis to bring that vision into reality. A key part of the business relationship is that open book accounting exists. The client knows exactly how much profit the contractor is receiving from providing the service.

As a model of the creative visioning process at work in creating a successful business partnership, the Peter Lane Transport–Body Shop example is outstanding.

Reference: BBC documentary, *Crazy Ways for Crazy Days*, featuring a Tom Peters Seminar in London.

California carried out research work on the human brain which led to the identification of two distinct types of mental processes. It has been known for some time that, if damage is done to the left hemisphere of the brain, the right side of the body tends to show signs of paralysis, and if damage is done to the right hemisphere of the brain, it is the left side of the body which seems to suffer. The research of Sperry and his colleagues has shown that these two different hemispheres of the brain seem to handle different mental activities. However, in biological terms they are similar and are best thought of as two identical brains working in harmony rather than as one brain divided into two parts.

Medical research using electroencephalograph (EEG) technology has shown that these two hemispheres handle different types of tasks. It is possible to measure the electrical activity in different parts of the brain when an individual is undertaking various types of task and the activity measured varies in location according to the types of task involved. Essentially, the tasks fall into two types in terms of the activity produced in the hemispheres of the brain. The following examples give some idea of how the two hemispheres differ in terms of the processes they handle:

Left hemisphere	*Right hemisphere*
Analysis	Synthesis and the whole picture
Logic	Rhythm
Lists	Colour and pictures
Sequence	Spatial awareness
Linearity	Imagination
Words	Daydreaming
Numbers	Dimensions
Rules	Intuition

One of the most interesting things that this split of mental processes reveals is that the conventional education system is heavily left brain-oriented, whilst the visioning process is inherently right-brain in nature. So it is no wonder that many people find the visioning process very challenging. There are, however, other factors involved. In Western society, and increasingly in the East, it is left brain-driven activity which is rewarded in organizations. People who spend their time daydreaming, creating mental images and working on the basis of intuition rather than logic are often thought lazy, irresponsible and lacking in drive, but, in reality, the opposite may be true. If we consider some of the geniuses in history, we can see that they were often right brain-oriented. Leonardo da Vinci was not only a good engineer, he was an artist capable of creating complex mental imagery and capturing that imagery on paper. Einstein is reputed to have thought up his Theory of Relatively while daydreaming about what it would be like to be travelling on a beam of light. You cannot get much more unconventional than that!

What do we make of all this left brain and right brain issue? The answer has to be in the realms of what we could call 'whole brain' thinking. Quite simply, we need to counter the tendency of our educational systems to focus mainly on left brain activity. We need to develop right brain skills as well and we now consider some of the ways of doing so.

Mind Mapping

This is a process which attempts to mirror what is believed to be the way the brain may handle complex information. There is much evidence to suggest that, whatever experiences a person has been subjected to, there is a memory of that experience recorded in the brain. Earlier this century, Wilder Penfield proved conclusively that memories can be stimulated during brain surgery even when the person concerned has no conscious awareness of the subject of the experience. This would suggest that the main problem an individual has regarding memory is more in the realms of data recall than data storage. Mind mapping is a process which seeks to improve the recall ability using a process of association. Created in the late 1960s by Tony Buzan, it has helped literally thousands of individuals to develop their mental skills in terms of memory and creativity.

In basic terms, the topic of the mind map is either written as a key word or displayed as a representative sketch at the centre of a blank sheet of paper, preferably in landscape orientation. The person then allows their mind to associate freely, putting down each idea as it arises rather than trying to create any logical sequence of ideas. With a little practice and a relaxed approach, the average person is often amazed at how much information can be represented on the mind in a short space of time. The trick is to use only key words and to keep writing rather than to try to evaluate the ideas as they arise. Figure 4.1 gives an idea of how a mind map may be generated, this time on leadership theory.

Starting a Mind Map on Leadership Theory

Note the lack of sequence of ideas – it is quantity which is important at this stage. Clients might be instructed as follows. Write or print the word first, then add the line to avoid using too much space. Relax and let the ideas come, no matter how disconnected they may appear. The messier the map the better – you can always apply logic later.

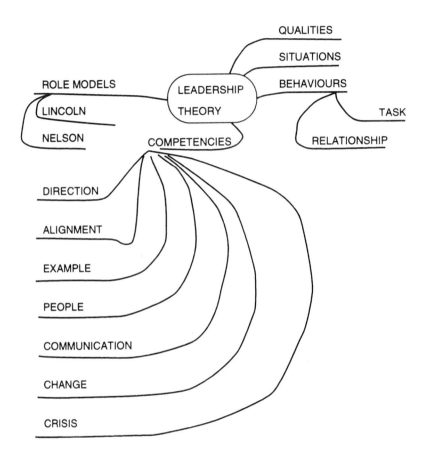

Figure 4.1   A sample mind map

Brainstorming

Brainstorming is perhaps the most well known of the deliberate approaches to tapping into the creative resources of a group of people. Essentially, the idea is to pull together a group of people to generate as many ideas as possible on solutions to a problem.

The best way to start a brainstorming session is to use a simple warm-up exercise, such as the following. First, the group of individuals involved should be seated around a table with a flip chart close by. One person should act as scribe to record all the ideas so that each individual around the table can see them. A simple everyday object such as a paper clip or coat hanger is then chosen as the warm-up subject. Each member of the group, including the scribe, puts forward any ideas that come to mind for the use of the object. The process seems to work best if the people around the table speak in turn so that everyone becomes involved. You might start with one person volunteering an idea and then move to the person on his or her left for their idea, then to the person on their left and so on to create a structured flow around the table. Once the process is under way, ideas can be presented by the group members in any sequence. The point about starting with a structured approach is that it ensures that everyone is involved at the beginning. Once the group has settled down and spent around five minutes on this process, it is ready to undertake the real brainstorming session on the matter at hand.

There are some key rules which should operate in a brainstorming session if the process is to work effectively. First, in its initial stage, the process is all about generating as many ideas as possible, regardless of their quality. It is important therefore never to criticize either ideas or people, because this tends to raise the tension level in the group and inhibit the creative process. Second, it is the quantity of ideas, however wild or crazy, which is important. What seems to happen is that, the more bizarre the ideas, the greater the chance of two or more of these combining to form a creative idea. As an example, the chemist who created *Post-It* notes was actually trying to create a really powerful adhesive. As such, his solution with the *Post-It* note was a failure, but rather than discard the idea of creating an adhesive that did not work very well, he started to explore the ideas of where such an adhesive could be useful. And so the *Post-It* note concept was born. Rather than discard apparently silly ideas, it is invariably useful to explore them to see if they trigger any creative ones.

Once a brainstorming session is under way, the ideas are generated very rapidly. The fact that they are recorded on a flip chart tends to reinforce the creative process, as constant exposure to the range of ideas often triggers unconscious thought processes and creates new ideas.

It is useful, sometimes, to take a break in a brainstorming session and focus attention on totally unrelated issues. The reason for this is that the creative process seems to work best when we are not trying to be creative! This is why we tend to become aware of good ideas, not when we are sitting at a desk trying to be creative, but when we are walking the dog, jogging, cleaning the car or some other activity where our unconscious processing faculties can operate in an uninhibited way. If we break off from the brainstorming process for a while, we allow the mind to incubate the ideas and their relationships and this makes for a complete list of possibilities.

Finally, we need to have some process of evaluating the ideas. Some will be useless and will be discarded, some will be possible but not exciting; and then there will be the useful ideas, which can be assessed and explored, after which a plan for their implementation can be created.

Multiple Perspectives

The idea of this approach is to create various viewpoints on a situation or vision. For example, we consider person A talking to person B, with person A having three possible perceptual positions. First, they can see the situation only from their personal viewpoint. This is what we call 'first position' and it is the perspective individuals tend to become mentally locked into. Second position is that of empathy, of seeing the situation from the other person's viewpoint. This is an important skill for any leader. Third position is that of the dissociated 'fly on the wall' which aims to remove personal emotion from the situation. Taken together, these three perceptual positions provide the leader with a useful way of gaining multiple perspectives on a situation.

Six Thinking Hats

This is a novel approach based on an idea from Edward de Bono, the well known writer on creativity and lateral thinking. The idea is that the leader adopts a specific approach to the thinking or visioning process according to one of six viewpoints. Each viewpoint is reflected by the leader adopting a particular 'hat'.

The white hat is for a perspective which is purely factual. From this perspective, the leader reviews purely factual information which can be substantiated. There are no opinions, no positive or negative interpretations and no emotional aspects considered. In contrast, the black hat is for a negative viewpoint on the situation. The leader deliberately considers the worst points about the situation and identities the problem areas with a negative interpretation of the likely outcomes. The blue hat relates to control aspects of the situation: identifying those aspects over which the leader and the team have control. To compensate for the black hat, the yellow hat is the optimistic viewpoint. This is where possible positive outcomes are maximized, where all the positive aspects of the situation are identified and where possibilities are viewed in as optimistic a light as possible. The green hat is the creative viewpoint. This perspective is based on the principal features of brainstorming already discussed: no idea is rejected as being impractical; no idea is evaluated. What matters is creating as many possibilities as the leader and the team can generate. The red hat is the emotional viewpoint. This is the highly subjective and, for some leaders, difficult area where feelings and emotions about the situation are explored.

Taken in isolation, none of these perspectives would provide an acceptable approach to a leadership problem, yet this is exactly the way many leaders often operate, for instance viewing a situation purely from a negative viewpoint or from a personal, emotional perspective – to name two common problems. However, taken together, these six perspectives can and do provide a very rich picture of a leadership challenge. As a part of the leader's toolkit, they are invaluable in providing a breadth of vision.

Submodalities

The approach of neurolinguistic programming (NLP) to the process of understanding human behaviour has already been mentioned. One of the key features of NLP is that it addresses the way individuals represent how they see the world around them in terms of their perceptual processes. In particular, NLP focuses on five sensory inputs: vision, sound, feeling, olfactory and gustatory. In the jargon of NLP, these are labelled V, A, K, O and G and are the sensory modes.

Submodalities are the specific aspects of the way the individual represents a situation in his or her mind in terms of these basic modes. The most commonly used modes are V, the visual, A the auditory and K the kinaesthetic. As an example, let us consider the visual mode. If we are exploring the submodalities of the way we represent a picture in our mind, namely a vision, we would be interested in the following:

- Is the picture in black and white or in colour?
- Is the picture bright or dim?
- Is it high-contrast and vivid or 'washed out'?
- Is the image sharp or fuzzy?
- Is the image detailed or general?
- Are the elements of the image large or small?
- How far away is the image?
- Are the shapes angular or round?
- Is there a border around the image or is it panoramic?
- Where is the image located – directly ahead or to the side?

By exploring these submodalities, we can gain a firm grasp of a specific vision. What is even more exciting is that, by changing some of the submodalities, we can often create a significant emotional impact. As an example, think of some event in your past that has given you pleasure.

Create an image in your mind which sums up that experience. Check out the image with the above questions. Is the image in black and white or in colour? Is there a frame around it? And so on. Then see what happens if you change one submodality at a time. If the picture is black and white, what happens if you make it coloured? If there is a frame around it, what happens if you make it panoramic? What happens if you make the elements larger? Try bringing the image closer. For most people, these particular submodality changes will intensify the positive emotions associated with the image.

So far we have only considered the visual aspect of submodalities. We can carry out the same process for both the auditory and the kinaesthetic aspects. The olfactory and gustatory aspects also lend themselves to exploration, although this tends to be less common than the basic V, A and K aspects. With sound, the idea is to explore the location of the sounds associated with the image. Do they come from behind or to one side? Are they loud or quiet? Is there an associated rhythm? With regard to the kinaesthetic aspects, what are the associated emotions and physical sensations that the vision creates? How strong are they? Is there movement associated with the vision? And so on. Submodalities enable the leader to explore in a scientific way and in depth the specifics of a vision. Furthermore, some of the submodalities will be more significant than others if they are changed. For example, if the image associated with a particular vision is brought nearer and the brightness increased, this may intensify the associated emotions considerably, whereas altering the other submodalities may have little effect. We call the significant submodalities that create such impact *key submodalities*. The interested reader is recommended to study the work of Richard Bandler for more details on the applications of submodalities particularly to the visioning process in terms of leadership. In particular, Bandler (1985) and Bandler and MacDonald (1988) provide an excellent guide to this fascinating aspect of the human perceptual processes.

Image streaming

This is a much less structured and scientific approach to the visioning process. In basic terms it is simply about clearing the mind and entering a state of relaxation. After a few minutes, the mind, normally active, will start to create a stream of images about both related and unrelated subjects. What is happening is that these images are presented by the unconscious in the absence of conscious thought processes.

In the middle of the twentieth century, psychologists began to explore the impact of sensory deprivation on the human brain. The person acting as a subject for the experiments was dressed in a waterproof suit and suspended in a tank of fluid at body temperature. The subject was blindfolded and 'white noise' (sound containing energy at all the audio frequencies) was played through headphones. The idea was to deprive the subject of the normal sensory inputs of sight, sound, touch, smell and taste. In a very short space of time, subjects began to hallucinate and produce their own images in the absence of external sensory inputs. The idea of image streaming is to encourage the internal generation of images without the paraphernalia or possible ethical problems associated with sensory deprivation. By simply relaxing and allowing the mind to generate images the person is tapping into the processes which have been used for years in many of the Eastern Buddhist communities. By stilling the conscious mind, the unconscious mind can present its contribution.

Developing Imagery

Many individuals claim that they do not have effective visioning or visual perceptual processes. However, if you ask them to describe a scene with which they are familiar, that description will be accurate! This means, of course, that they must have some visual representation. The problem is one of understanding what we actually mean by 'vision' or 'image'. There are some exercises which may be used very effectively to raise an individual's awareness of the images they can create. For example, one such exercise is simply to look at the cover of a book and then close one's eyes and focus on the image created of the book cover. Because of the way the eye processes its inputs, there will be a residual image of the book cover and this serves to increase the confidence of the individual concerned in terms of their perception of their ability to visualize effectively.

Another simple exercise is for the individual to think of a scene, perhaps a room in their house, and imagine walking around that room, hearing the associated sounds and touching specific objects. With a little ingenuity and some practice, even the most non-visual individual can develop some surprisingly effective visioning and visualization skills.

What is Not Perfect Yet: 20 Ideas for Improvement

In the latter part of the twentieth century, the Japanese have contributed much to the way we believe quality organizations should function. In particular, the Kaizen approach is valuable in that it focuses on incremental rather than revolutionary change in terms of improvement. The idea is to think of terms of doing a thousand things one per cent better, rather than one thing a thousand per cent better. This is very relevant to the visioning process, particularly where detail is concerned. As with problem solving and solution finding in general, the aim is to assess the present situation, consider what is required instead of that situation and then create a process for achieving that transition. Thus the creation of the vision of the desired state is a vital part of the solution-finding process. One way of achieving this effectively is to consider creating 20 ways of improving the present situation and moving towards the required state. What usually happens during this process is that the individual finds it relatively easy to think up seven or eight ideas. Then the sensible ideas seem to dry up. On being pressed to contribute more ideas, the person is forced to propose either impractical or nonsensical thoughts. This usually takes the list up to around a dozen or so. Then something surprising tends to happen: all of a sudden, a stupid idea will often create a sensible, high-quality one. This is the basis of true creativity.

It has often been said that there is little new in the universe. What we are doing when we are being creative is linking two or more ideas which have not been previously linked rather than creating any new ideas. With our list of improvement suggestions, it seems that the non-practical ideas play a key role in triggering unusual ideas in the mind and thus creating these novel linkages of ideas. Thus being 'silly' is a vital part of being creative.

The ideas created from number 12 to 20 are often high-quality, creative approaches to the situation. The reason for limiting the number to 20 is purely practical. The main aim of the exercise is to break through the 'being sensible' barrier to tap into the creative potential of the person and this happens midway through the list.

In reality, when an individual creates such a list many of the ideas will not work out in practice. The present authors' experience in this respect is that probably only two of the ideas will be workable and capable of implementation – and only one of these ideas will be sustainable. However, it is invariably the case that one idea will work out and it is this idea which is the pearl in the oyster. If an individual in an organization carried out this exercise once a week and contributed one new idea for improvement, this would be over forty ideas per year. In an organization of a thousand individuals, imagine the impact of 40 000 new ideas for improvement in a year. Leadership through effective visioning and Kaizen is powerful.

Summary

In this chapter we have explored the important aspect of leadership vision. We have taken a slightly unusual approach by looking at the specific skills involved in terms of developing the ability to create visions of the future. The issue of communication of that vision has also been explored as it is a vital part of the leadership process. Sperry's work on the left and right hemispheres of the brain led us to the concept of mind mapping as a tool for creative visioning. Brainstorming and multiple perspectives also offer much to the leader as ways of thinking creatively about creating a vision and setting the direction for the future. However, it is the area of neurolinguistic programming which offers the most in terms of specific tools for developing the skills of leadership excellence. Although still in its early days, NLP has transformed many lives and offers both a philosophy for understanding human experience and a range of tools for putting that philosophy into practice. With these skills of effective visioning, our leaders of the future will have much to offer the rest of the human race.

References

Bandler, R. (1985), 'Using Your Brain – for a CHANGE', Utah: Real People Press.
Bandler, R. and MacDonald, W. (1988), *An Insider's Guide to Submodalities*, Meta Publications.
Sashkin, M. (1986), *How to Become a Visionary Leader*, Bryn Mawr, PA: Organization Design and Development Inc.

5   Leadership and the Individual

The Importance of the Individual

We have seen in the latter part of the twentieth century a major trend towards the creation of effective teams in our organizations. Indeed, the next chapter of this book is devoted to that very subject. However, before discussing the impact of leadership on the team it is important to acknowledge that teams are made up of individuals. It is possible to raise the performance of individuals from mediocre to good in a team context. If, however, we also work on the development of the individuals within the team, it is possible to raise the performance level to excellent and beyond. One of the great strengths of John Adair's 'three circles' approach to leadership is that it emphasizes the point that the leader needs to take account of the 'people needs' in a situation by working at both the team and the individual level. In this chapter we explore the nature of the individual and the impact of effective leadership. Leadership is largely an emotional process. As Carl Jung is reported to have said, 'There can be no transforming of darkness into light and of apathy into movement without emotion'. As leadership is a transformational process, we do need to understand what makes the individual 'tick' in order to trigger that process.

A powerful insight into the approach to transforming the individual and tapping into what in many instances can be a wealth of knowledge and skill was given by one Japanese chief executive in June 1985. Talking about the apparent shift in terms of intellectual leadership in many areas, K. Matsushita was quoted in the UK newspaper, the *Daily Telegraph*, as saying about the East:

> We are going to win and the industrial West is going to lose because for you the essence of management is getting ideas out of the heads of bosses into the hands of labour. For us the core of management is the art of mobilising and putting together the intellectual resources of all employees in the services of the firm.

This is an interesting perspective because it reflects the shift from autocratic to facilitative leadership we have already mentioned and because it really does sum up the nature of transformational leadership. It is about tapping into the intellectual resources of everyone in the organization rather than relying on one person, the leader, to have all the answers.

As a way of justifying our view that the individual is becoming increasingly important, it is worth reflecting on what appears to be a trend in many organizations. In the 1960s and 1970s, the emphasis was on the task aspect of individuals. 'Management by objectives' became a much favoured style of management. Business school course programmes seemed to work hard at removing the emotion from business and emphasizing the 'hard issues' of finance, strategy and return to investors. However, in the 1980s, with the sudden increase in the rate of change due to a whole range of factors, there was a gradual trend towards acknowledging that people were important and that they performed most effectively within a team context. Tom Peters and Robert Waterman played a key part in the shift of this emphasis with *In Search of Excellence* (1982). It was the chapter headings which attracted such attention when the book was published. The authors talked in terms of customers, productivity through people, hands-on value-driven activity and leadership rather than the more conventional 'hard issues' of finance, strategy and systems. Subsequently, however, this philosophy ran into difficulties as a number of the examples of organizations quoted as excellent failed to perform as well as predicted in the mid-1980s. People's Express was just one company which seemed set for stardom but disappeared fairly rapidly, for a variety of reasons. Those reasons do not concern us in this chapter; what is important is that the fundamental problem with the Peters and Waterman approach is that it assumed a static model of excellence. In essence, it was built upon a list of attributes: if an organization worked towards creating and displaying those attributes than it would be both 'excellent' and successful. History proved otherwise! Peters has commented many times on this issue. His point is essentially that the research for *In Search of Excellence* was carried out in the 1970s when the world seemed a much more stable and predictable place.

Since the early 1980s, the business world in particular has seen an incredible escalation in the rate of change. It is this rate of change which is addressed in Tom Peters' *Thriving on Chaos* (1987). This text, in the words of its author, is essentially a 'handbook for a management revolution'. It focuses on two key issues: how management can operate in such a way as to embrace and thrive on change, and ways of tapping into the inherent abilities of the workforce at all levels. The interesting point as far as this chapter is concerned is that the emphasis is undoubtedly on triggering the individual. People do seem to operate more effectively when they interact with others, with the result that the team approach is invariably cited as the way to promote increased levels of effectiveness.

However, despite the team approach having been in existence for over a decade in many organizations, there is little formal evidence to suggest that simply putting people into teams is the end of the story. Despite the sophisticated approaches to creating effective team structures and the diagnostic tools which now exist, many teams simply do not reach their potential. It is this aspect which is now shifting attention towards the individual within the team. And here we can return to some basic leadership theory, in particular the functional or action-centred approach of John Adair. We have seen in the past decade a shift from an emphasis on the task to an emphasis on the team and now to an emphasis on the individual.

Yet Another Leadership Paradox

Once we identify that the individual is important, we encounter another leadership paradox. Throughout this book, we have been suggesting that leadership is more about a process created by an individual interacting with a team than the focus on the individual leader. However, there needs to be more awareness of the impact of that process on the individual as well as the team. It is simply a matter of a shift of emphasis about which individual we are looking at, in terms of the leadership process. Instead of concentrating on the qualities and characteristics of the leader, we now want to consider the impact of the process on the individual followers and how that process may be improved.

What Makes People Tick?

There are many models of motivation which provide us with a starting point to consider how the leader affects the individual. We have already considered, in Chapter 3, Maslow's hierarchy approach. This would suggest that the leader operates by providing the potential for the satisfaction of human needs. At the lowest level of operation, the leader is seen as being able to create a situation where the individual's basic survival needs are met. The emphasis then moves to the leader being in a position to provide some degree of safety. Once this is satisfied to a significant extent, the focus shifts to creating a social network and satisfying belonging needs. This, in turn, leads to individuals wanting to feel important in terms of self-esteem and then to Maslow's highest order of need, that of self-actualization. As a concept, self-actualization is interesting both in its own right and in relation to the leadership process. It might be argued that what effective leadership really does is to shift individual followers into their own specific self-actualization state where they are capable of achieving more of their potential. If we take the notion that leadership is a transformational process, then the role of the leader in helping people to self-actualize is obvious.

It is appropriate here to say a word about the growth of terrorism in the latter part of the twentieth century in relation to leadership and Maslow's 'hierarchy of needs'. The terrorist aims to undermine the population's belief in the leadership of the country by attacking systems at the very low level of safety and security needs. It is difficult for a country to grow and develop if individuals are constantly focusing on the lower order needs instead of those closer to self-actualization.

As well as Maslow, the approaches of other established writers on motivation, such as Douglas McGregor and Frederick Herzberg, are relevant. McGregor proposed the idea that individual managers tend to fall into two categories as far as expectations of the performance of their subordinates was concerned. There are those managers who believe people are basically lazy and need to be bullied into action; these are what McGregor termed 'Theory X' managers. There are also those managers who believe that their people are capable of great things and only need to be given the tools to do the job and sufficient encouragement in order for them to perform at a high level' this is what McGregor termed 'Theory Y' management. It is quite clear that Theory Y is just another way of looking at transformational leadership; that is, the process of developing people so that they operate at a level nearer to their true potential.

What Herzberg said was that the factors that motivated individuals were not the same as the factors that demotivated them. He talked in terms of 'motivators' and 'hygiene factors'. Motivators included such issues as achievement and the recognition of those achievements, a sense of growing as an individual, an interesting job and responsibility. If motivator issues are dealt with successfully in the organization, the individual will produce enhanced performance; if they are not handled effectively, the individuals will not necessarily be demotivated but, quite simply, they will only produce mediocre, lacklustre results.

'Hygiene factors', on the other hand, include such issues as organizational policy, supervision, work conditions, salary, relationships with peers, status and security issues. If these factors are not dealt with in a satisfactory way, individuals will become demotivated. On the other hand, even if an enormous amount of resources is poured into hygiene factors, the level of motivation produced will be modest. Thus the things that demotivate if they are wrong are not the same as those that motivate if they are right. The key to motivation once again shows itself as the transformation process.

It is thus useful to remind ourselves of Herzberg's motivator factors: achievement, recognition of achievement, the nature of the work, responsibility, advancement and personal growth. The theme is simple. Whatever conventional model of motivation is considered, it is the leader who 'switches people on'; that is, he is the one who creates a motivated, transformed individual.

We can relate the three established models of Maslow, McGregor and Herzberg to each other: 'Theory X' management relates to lower-order needs and 'Theory Y' is more aligned to the satisfaction of higher-order needs, including self-esteem and self-actualization; 'hygiene factors' relate to lower-order needs and motivators to the higher-order needs. There is undoubtedly a common theme that enables us to integrate at least three of the established views on motivation.

Developing a Model of the Individual

The established models of motivation do not really give us more than a superficial understanding of what makes people tick, particularly in relation to the way the leader influences individuals. We need to look to the discipline of psychology and, in particular, some of the more revolutionary ideas on how the individual operates. One far-reaching development in recent years, as we have already mentioned, has been the development of the technology of neurolinguistic programming (NLP), which is somewhat of an enigma and an embarrassment to the psychological and psychiatric professions.

What Grinder and Bandler attempted to do was to model human excellence. They studied a number of key individuals who had risen to the top in terms of their personal performance and then they attempted to 'unpack' how those individuals were successful. The mostly commonly quoted individuals were Milton Erickson, a noted hypnotherapist and physician, Virginia Satir, who was a family therapist, and Gregory Bateson, a philosopher and systems thinker.

Since the 1970s, NLP has assumed almost a religious devotion on the part of its followers and this has done much to alienate the technology from the established conventional psychological disciplines. However, the fact remains that, in the hands of a competent practitioner, NLP works! An individual with effective NLP skills can often cure client phobias in less than an hour, whilst conventional therapy can take months, and some individuals, on exposure to the ideas of NLP, suddenly seem to transform their lives to become both happier and more effective. It is therefore easy to see how NLP has almost gained religious status in the eyes of some individuals. However, we need to take a balanced viewpoint in deciding which parts of NLP, if any, are relevant to the leadership situation. The interested reader is referred to the excellent *Introduction to Neurolinguistic Programming* (1990) by Joseph O'Connor and John Seymour.

For our purposes in this chapter on the individual, the most relevant part of NLP is the model of the individual shown in Figure 5.1. The concept of this was initially proposed by Robert Dilts and then developed by John Potter, one of the present authors, to provide a diagnostic model for individuals in terms of their development. This is an elegant model in that it provides a representation of the human being in a two-dimensional form. In doing so, it integrates a number of psychological concepts which have been presented quite separately until now.

It is suggested that, at the core of each individual, is a concept of who they are and how they see themselves. This identity appears to be at the core of the psychology of each individual. Effective leaders often seem to have an intense self concept and cannot conceive of themselves as being anything

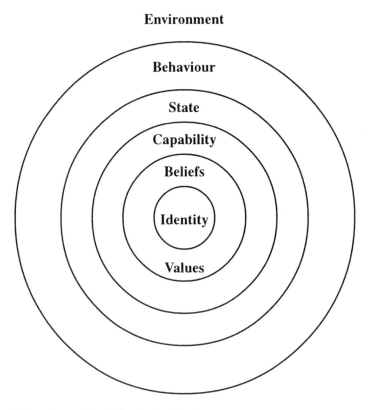

Figure 5.1   A model of the individual

other than the leader! History abounds with examples of such people: Napolean, Nelson, Alexander the Great, Adolf Hitler, Abraham Lincoln, Margaret Thatcher and Nelson Mandela are just some of the people who spring to mind. It is often this seeing themselves as a leader which is the key to the motivation of some of these figures who have had a tremendous impact on the human race – some of it positive and some of it less so.

Beliefs and Values

Surrounding the core concept of identity is the important area of beliefs and values. Beliefs relate to the framework of what we believe about the nature of the job, what we can or cannot do, the issues we can control and influence and a whole range of issues relating to the way we operate on a day-to-day basis.

The possession of limiting beliefs seems to be the main factor which holds people back. Changing those beliefs into empowering ones is a challenging but not impossible task. This is the level at which effective leaders seem to operate. We all have reference experiences which support our beliefs. If a leader can encourage people to reframe negative experiences in such a way that they see them as learning experiences then limiting beliefs can be shifted. The problem with beliefs is that most human beings are skewed towards a negative interpretation of events. We see in a situation what we want to see. If leaders want to develop people and empower them, they have to enable them to develop a set of positive beliefs about themselves and their work.

The values issue is another important area: what do we really feel is important in terms of how we operate? If we now relate this to leadership, we can see that, if a leader wants to produce 'transformed individuals', it is vital that those individuals experience a shift in their sense of identity in such a way that they feel capable of enhanced performance. Coupled with this, and the set of beliefs about themselves and their job just discussed, they need a sound awareness of what is truly important in the way that they operate.

The Self Concept

The areas of identity, beliefs and values define what Rogers (1969) called the self concept – the sense of who a person feels they are in terms of their ability to operate effectively and have an impact on other people – and it is this self concept which defines what a person is capable of achieving. One of the key elements of the self concept is the idea of self-esteem: how much people like themselves. People with high self-esteem tend to perform better than those who undervalue themselves. If a leader is to transform his or her people, it is vital that attention is paid to boosting the self-esteem of the individuals if the aim is truly to tap into their potential.

Self concept defines capability. How much of that capability can be accessed depends on the state in which the individual finds himself on a daily basis. This 'transmission' of capability to behaviour is important in a whole range of human behaviour. For example, for some years now, time management experts have been saying that being too busy is a state of mind – we always have time to do the things which are truly important to us. This links behaviour to the issue of both beliefs and values.

Much of leadership at the present time is concerned with the process of empowerment. This is particularly true in terms of leadership for the future. One of the issues which is particularly valid and important in an empowerment context is the notion of powerless. Peters has said recently that 'powerlessness is a state of mind. If you think you're powerless, you are' (Peters, 1994). Perhaps we should recall the Henry Ford statement of many years ago: 'If you think you can or you think you can't, you're probably right.' Empowerment really is about producing a shift in mind-set from organizational learned helplessness to a burning desire to do something and to make a difference. Once again, this is the basis of transformational leadership.

The amount of his or her capability that an individual can tap into depends on the state in which they find themselves, both physical and psychological, and this is where the important skill of operating under pressure becomes relevant. Stress has become an important topic in the workplace in recent years. When individuals feel that they cannot cope with the changes demanded by, for example, an empowerment initiative, the resultant stress can lead to poor performance, accidents and absenteeism. The cost of stress-related problems in the workplace runs into billions of pounds annually in the UK. Development and training for empowerment must involve giving people skills to enable them to cope with the pressures and stress associated with change.

Where Behaviour Fits In

State defines actual behaviour or the part of our capability which we can access. A poor state will lead to poor performance, regardless of inherent capability. And it is actual behaviour which enables the individual to affect his or her environment. Behaviour is the observable output of the individual. It is that part of the individual's operation which we can see and which can be measured. Other aspects of the individual are open to highly subjective interpretation. For example, it requires considerable ability on the part of a manager or leader to elicit an individual's beliefs or value set, while behaviour can be readily observed. This is why, in the 1960s, many leadership models were about leader behaviour. Probing leader identity, or such issues as beliefs and values, was not deemed scientific; behaviour, on the other hand, can be observed and recorded. The problem with this approach is that it leaves out the very essence of leadership, the emotional transformational aspect.

To understand the total operation of a leader it is important that we consider not only the behavioural aspects but also the identity, beliefs, values, capability and state aspects. In short, we need to take a holistic approach.

The Holistic Leader

If we want a leader to produce lasting results, we have to take into account all these levels on which an individual operates. Leaders have to ensure that they create in the followers a clear identity and sense of personal focus with a set of empowering beliefs to help in their ability to overcome the inevitable problems they will confront. Followers and leaders need a clear sense of values so that they can work together and prioritize their workload effectively.

Each individual needs to develop a sense of their strengths and areas for development and this is where 'contractor mind-set' – by which we mean the ability of an individual to see themselves in terms of the value they add rather than as simply filling an organizational 'slot' – becomes even more relevant. It is often said that the acid test of 'contractor mind-set' is to imagine that you have been made redundant by the organization and taken on as a contractor. Ask yourself what you are going to be stating on your invoice as the 'services rendered' or value added. Many managers holding onto an 'employee mind-set' find this difficult. It is, however, a vital exercise bearing in mind the ways organizations will be structured in the future. More than anything else, mind-set influences an individual's capability. This in turn is linked very strongly to beliefs and identity. Converting potential and capability into specific action must take into account the culture of the organization and the extent to which individuals feel they can cope effectively with the demands made upon them. It is important that we take into account all these levels of individual operation if we are to avoid the problem of the 'quick fix', the effects of which last for only a short period.

In effect, this is a holistic model of leadership and it is one which operates not simply at the behavioural level. It leads us to what has become a theme in terms of management operation in the 1990s; that is, the process of redefining the role of the manager away from boss and towards that of coach. Management coaching has become fashionable and has much to commend it in terms of shifting the culture of the organization. In many respects, organizations are like people: some are aggressive, some are defensive, and some manage their energy in a constructive way. It is this constructive redirection of energy, away from internal politics of interdepartmental conflict and risk avoidance towards constructive cooperation, which is the challenge for the leader of the future. How is this achieved? The answer to this question is in the holistic approach to leadership in terms of the corporate culture which exists in an organization.

The Implications of Holistic Leadership for Corporate Culture

There are four factors which seem to shift organizational cultures by changing the perceptions of individuals in terms of how they operate on a day-to-day basis. First, individuals who have set goals seem to be more focused in the way they operate and behave. Thus, in terms of transforming individuals, the role of the leader in guiding, encouraging and agreeing goals with individuals is paramount. Second, individuals who feel that they are growing and developing as people seem to concentrate their energy on constructive pursuits rather than on internal politics. The role of the leader of the future is thus geared very much towards what Maslow calls 'self-actualization'. The third issue relates to individuals developing a wide perception of where they fit in to the organization and to developing cross-functional activity rather than what Peters calls 'functional turf guarding'. In the past, many organizations have encouraged individuals to develop their operation almost at the expense of other departments. In the future, individuals will need to focus on how the value they add benefits the organization as a whole, rather than just their own immediate area of responsibility. The fourth factor we have identified is that of the 'atmosphere' within the organization being one which acknowledges that individuals do acquire problems and that counselling is a valid activity. And this extends to coaching: effective organizations seem to have a feel about them that coaching and counselling activity is valuable in that it improves relationships and develops the organization as a whole.

The Leader as Coach

We will now look in some detail at the skills of coaching. In particular, we need to identify what leaders are required to do if they are to coach effectively and move from autocrat to facilitator and enabler. One of the most concise definitions of coaching is that it is using day-to-day work as learning experiences. Thus it does not suffer the same intrinsic cost or artificiality as conventional training. However, there is a subtle issue that we need to address at this stage. There is a difference in mental approach on the part of the individual being trained from that of the individual being coached. In most cases, training implies that the individual is in some way less expert at the subject area than the trainer or, in this case, the leader. Individuals undergoing the training process usually do not have a strong image of themselves as being expert at the area being trained. They are prepared to admit that there is room for development on their part.

The same in not true for coaching. In fact, some of the most effective coaches are not as proficient at the skill or topic as the person being coached. Essentially, the coaching process is about providing constructive feedback on the actual performance level of the individual, not simply telling them how to perform. A coach is actually dealing with an individual who has some form of positive self-image as regards their ability to perform the skill or task. Thus coaching is as much about managing self-esteem and self-image on the part of the person being coached as it is about the content of the performance. This does not mean that coaches have to take a 'soft' line in terms of how they deal with the individual being coached: the management of self-esteem can be achieved through challenge as well as through encouragement. What is important is that the person being coached trusts the coach and has belief in their ability to produce the required results.

There are two types of coaching as far as the leader is concerned. The first type is reactive coaching, which is often practised by managers even if they do not recognize it as such. Reactive coaching occurs in response to a work problem. The manager or leader identifies an individual who would benefit from the experience of working on and solving the particular problem. In this situation, it is the nature of the problem task which determines the areas of development experienced by the individual.

The second, more sophisticated, type of coaching is called proactive coaching. This involves much more in the way of a planning process. The competencies, strengths and areas for development of the individual being coached are first considered in terms of the actual and desired performance levels. Opportunities are then sought to provide development in these specific areas. Thus the process focuses much more on the needs of the person being coached and it is this aspect of needs which is the basis for the coaching activity.

Coaching does not just benefit the person being coached: it develops the coach or leader as well. Relationships with subordinates are developed, more effective delegation occurs and, above all, development occurs on the part of the coach in terms of his or her understanding of the nature of the skill being coached. Stephen Covey identified this fact in his *Seven Habits of Highly Effective People* (1989). He advises aspiring individuals to study, practise and then teach the material to others as a way of maximizing their own self-development. Maybe there is a moral here for the aspiring leader or, as we would suggest, the learning leader.

Our model for proactive coaching is a straightfoward approach to the subject. First, it is important to identify the needs of the job: just what does the individual need to be good at to perform the task to a defined high standard? This then leads to an identification of the areas in which that individual could benefit from some development activity. The leader then looks for specific opportunities to develop those areas. This is where proactive coaching differs from reactive coaching. It is the needs of the individual and identifying specific opportunities related to those needs rather than general development which distinguish proactive coaching from reactive coaching.

A model which seems to sum up the principles of effective proactive coaching is shown as Figure 5.2. Reactive coaching follows a similar process in terms of briefing and feedback but lacks the skill component analysis aspect. If we consider the full proactive coaching process, the first stage is to consider the individual in terms of the skills and competencies required for them to perform well at the job.

The person to be coached is then briefed so that they undertake the task in as strong a position as possible as regards potential outcomes. Next, the action or event takes place and the leader appraises the learning. And it is here that the maintenance and development of self-esteem is so important. The coach needs to start the debriefing session by focusing on the positive aspects of the performance. Provided this appraisal is sincere, it creates a good feeling on the part of the person being coached. Attention then moves to the areas for development. It is a good idea at this stage to ask the person being coached for their appraisal of their performance. Individuals being coached are often harder on themselves than would be an external observer. The coach can bond more effectively with the individual by countering self-doubt and offering encouragement. Handled effectively, coaching can produce significant performance improvement by providing objective feedback. As a process, it works most effectively when it is working at the beliefs level in terms of developing the confidence of the individual being coached.

Coaching has been an established part of the sports world for many decades and it is interesting to link the role of the managers with that of the sports coach. Traditionally, managers have been involved in such issues as

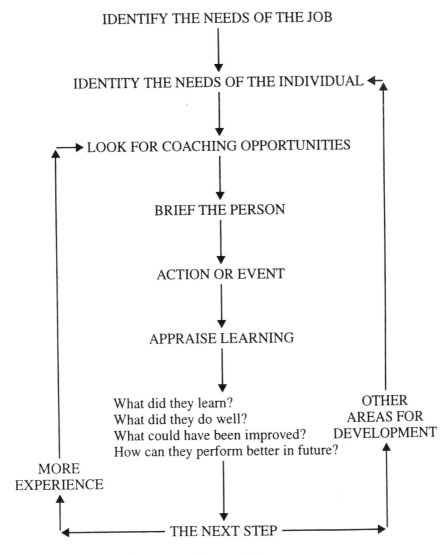

Figure 5.2   A model for proactive coaching

financial planning, quality control, productivity, planning and managing human resources, which has often included both training and supervision. We are now suggesting that there is an opportunity to develop this human resources role by coaching and then delegating some of these prime management tasks to the rest of the workforce. Carried out effectively, this can free up the time of the manager and leader and allow them to concentrate on more strategic issues.

It is worth pausing at this stage to reflect on what we mean by individual development, on the part both of the leader and of the person to be coached. There are two graphical approaches which may be useful here. The first relates to the extent to which the individual satisfies the requirement of the job. In Figure 5.3, we can see that a person partly fills the requirement of the job. The challenge for the leader is twofold: first, how to develop the individual so that he or she more closely fits the demands of the current job – this objective may be achieved by training, coaching, education and a whole variety of other means varying in terms of financial cost and time commitment on the part of the leader; second, what happens when the individual fully accomplishes the job requirement? Like companies, individuals do not stand still – they either expand or contract. Thus the leader is faced with the task of finding ways to enhance, enrich and generally 'grow' the job if the individual is to continue to grow.

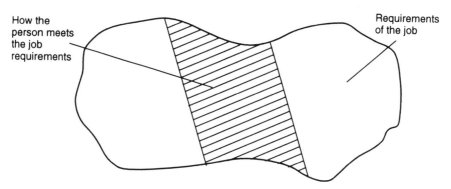

Figure 5.3   Map of the job

A slightly different issue occurs with Figure 5.4. It is being argued increasingly by many individuals that human beings are almost unlimited in terms of what they can achieve. If we accept this idea, there is no limit to the potential boundary on Figure 5.4. The leader may have to come to terms with the fact that sometimes individuals will develop to such an extent that the leader is no longer the appropriate person to lead them. In fact, it could be said that one measure of a coach's success is the performer's outgrowing the coach's ability to coach him or her. So what are the principal activities for the coach to take into consideration? There are six:

1   set targets and goals;
2   build rapport and develop the relationship;
3   motivate the person being coached and manage morale;
4   provide specific training input and guidance;
5   monitor the actual performance;
6   provide objective feedback.

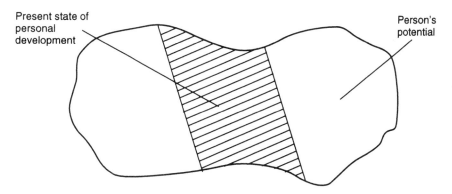

Present state of
personal
development

Person's
potential

Figure 5.4   Map of the person

All this is vital activity if we are to shift the role of the manager from boss towards the Matsushita concept, cited at the start of the chapter, of facilitator and enabler. So why is it that managers do not coach enough? We have asked many managers this question and it appears that there are four main reasons. First, there is the lack of time; it is invariably quicker and less risky to do the task oneself rather than invest the time in developing the ability of a subordinate. Second, many organizations still do not promote a 'coaching culture'. Managers are rewarded primarily for getting the job done rather than for developing people and this is invariably reflected in the operational situation when the workload is heavy. A third excuse revolves around the promotion issue. Many managers do not see the point in developing their people if no opportunities for promotion exist. This is a wider issue than one might at first think. In the West, we have suffered from 'promotionitis' for some time. Success is equated with moving up the corporate ladder rather than developing in the current position. With increasingly flat structures, we cannot continue to hold this view if we are to become world class.

There is a fourth reason why many managers do not coach effectively: they lack the basic skills and the awareness of how to put those skills into practice. They are so busy 'fire fighting' that they simply are not oriented to the human resource development issue in terms of their own teams. This is a classic example of short-termism pushing strategic issues into the back-ground – and coaching is very much a strategic issue as well as an opera-tional one. If the manager and leader develop their people through effective coaching then there will be more time available for the all-important strate-gic issues on which many managers spend precious little time.

Effective Goal Setting

Of all the skills involved in coaching, goal setting is perhaps the most important. On a basic psychological level, there is an enormous amount of evidence to suggest that individuals who have clearly defined goals tend to be more effective. Perhaps the most impressive evidence in this respect relates to a Yale University study on goal setting carried out in 1953. The graduating class was asked who had written goals for their careers and their lives. Only 3 per cent of the group had taken the trouble to think about and write down their goals. When this group was investigated some 20 years later, the 3 per cent who had written goals were worth more in financial terms that the other 97 per cent added together! Not only were the goal setters richer in financial terms, there were fewer incidences of divorce, they suffered less in the way of ill-health and were happier in a host of ways. Goal setting really does make a difference.

There are two basic ideas we have to remember when setting a goal: we must be specific and we need to develop the skills of what could be called 'total vision' – we need to develop the ability to imagine the goal as if it had already been achieved, and we need to see, hear and feel the desired result as if it were already present.

One approach to goal setting which seems to have stood the test of time is the SMART approach. The mnemonic stands for the goal being specific, measurable, attainable, realistic/relevant and time-bounded. This is certainly useful as a quick check on the quality of our goal, but it lacks the all-important aspect of 'total vision'. There is no emotion in the SMART approach. Truly effective goals become embedded in the unconscious mind of the individual and set up behaviours so that the goal becomes almost a self-fulfilling prophecy. The best way to approach effective goal setting for both oneself and the individual being coached is to use a combination of the SMART approach and 'total vision'.

There is an issue we need to address at this stage. The above approach to setting goals is highly effective. Thus it is vital that any individual who sets about creating a goal understands fully both the process of working towards achieving the goal and being able to live with the consequences once it is achieved. There are two safeguards the leader needs to build into the process both for themselves and for any individuals with whom they might be undertaking the process. First, goal setting is basically a creative process and as such needs to be undertaken in such a way that many options are considered before the final goal is decided upon. The basic principles of divergent and then convergent thinking are both needed. We need to use divergent thinking to open our minds to the possibilities and then convergent thinking to decide on the appropriate goal and how to create a plan to bring it into reality.

Second, an individual goal should be part of a strategy and not isolated because individuals who have just one goal tend to become obsessed with it. This is not psychologically healthy and invariably leads to distorted viewpoints on not only the goal but other issues as well. Thus goal setting should be seen as a three-stage process: possibility thinking, creation of a goal matrix and writing the goal in a SMART and 'total vision' format. The easiest way to approach the first stage is simply to brainstorm on an individual or group basis ideas under three main headings:

| *All the things you want to BE* | *All the things you want to DO* | *All the things you want to HAVE* |

Although this is a relatively simple process, it does create a range of options in three vital areas: it addresses the issue of personal development in terms of attributes, qualities and other issues relating to the all-important identity issue; it focuses on actual behaviours; and it considers the material and resource issues.

Once the basic set of possibilities is created, the idea is to select the three most significant goal areas under each heading. This will give the person a total of nine areas on which to work, the maximum number that can be handled effectively. Having created the list of nine goal areas, the next stage is to fit these goals into a goal matrix. This is essentially a chart with goal areas along the horizontal axis and timescales down the left-hand side, as in Table 5.1. In this example, six areas only are shown. The actual headings will, of course, be determined by the actual goal areas. This can be best achieved by asking yourself a number of questions, as in Table 5.2. Goals that are cycled through this process become embedded in the unconscious of the individual and invariably seem to be transferred into reality.

Goals that are set using this three stage process are powerful. They use a creative approach linked to a logical strategy and then are translated into specific actions. They thus form a significant part of the leader's array of tools for influencing the individual.

Table 5.1   The goal matrix

	Goal areas					
	Work	Family	Leisure	Finance	Travel	Relationships
1 month						
6 months						
1 year						
3 years						
5 years						
10 years						
Life						

Table 5.2   The power of effective goal setting

What do I want to achieve?
How can I create two ways of representing my goal visually?
Why do I want to achieve it?
How can I give myself leverage to achieve the goal?
What benefits would I gain by achieving the goal?
What pain would I avoid by achieving this goal?
When do I want to achieve it?
Is it realistic and relevant?
Is it attainable?
If I had achieved it, what would I see?
If I had achieved it, what would I hear?
If I had achieved it, what sensations would I experience externally?
How would I feel internally?
How specifically will I go about the task?
What first step can I take right now?
Why have I not achieved this goal yet?
What roadblocks can I anticipate along the way?
Which of my personal qualities do I need to strengthen in order to reach the
  goal?
Do I really want to achieve this goal?
Who else will it affect?
What resources will I need?

Summary

Leadership is about emotion. It is about transforming people at the individual level by creating an emotional impact and then transforming identity. It is about replacing limiting beliefs with empowering ones, clarifying values, developing capability and then creating effective states both in organizational terms and on the individual level. In this chapter we have considered some of the approaches to understanding the nature of the individual. We have looked at the established approaches of Maslow, Herzberg and McGregor and also at the somewhat controversial approach of NLP. We have seen how a sense of identity and a set of beliefs and values creates an individual's self concept. This, in conjunction with capability created by knowledge and resources, elicits an individual's potential. This potential may be tapped into using effective state or stress control and this results in behaviour which in turn affects the whole environment in which the individual operates. As we move into an uncertain future, it may be the increased understanding on the part of the leader of what makes the individual 'tick' which will hold one of the great secrets of success.

References

Covey, S.R. (1989), *The 7 Habits of Highly Effective People*, New York: Simon & Schuster.

O'Connor, J. and Seymour, J. (1990), *Introducing Neuro-Linguistic Programming*, London: Mandala.

Peters, T.J. (1987), *Thriving on Chaos*, London: Macmillan.

Peters, T.J. (1994), *The Tom Peters Seminar*, New York: Vintage Books.

Peters, T.J. and Waterman, R.H. (1982), *In Search of Excellence*, New York: Harper & Row.

Rogers, C. (1969), *On Becoming a Person*, London: Constable.

6 Leadership and Teams

Leaders and Followers

The relationship between leaders and teams has always been a fascinating area and it has also been subjected to considerable study. Until recently, the accepted view of this relationship has been based on the premise of a leader being set apart from the followers. This is due to a number of factors, ranging from the traditional role of rulers in the past to the position today of those in autocratic positions at the head of hierarchies (such as dictators and a number of the world's military, police and business leaders). This autocratic role of the leader has been accepted by followers for centuries and is borne out by the oft-repeated statement that 'leaders are born, not made'. There are many who still believe this, despite its unproven validity. However, even those who most easily fall into this category, such as hereditary sovereigns or dynastic political and business leaders, had to be taught how to become a leader during their adolescence – and there are many examples of those apparently 'born to lead' who subsequently failed miserably.

The epitome of the autocrat is the solo 'hero' leader. This is the one in whom all power is vested and from whom all decisions flow. To such an individual, information is power and therefore it is restricted to a small circle of people whom the leader trusts. It is the antithesis of empowerment and therefore, in this age of increasing democracy, it should become increasingly outdated.

Such is the theory, but in practice, this is not the case. Even today, people still want to be led. As an example, it is clear that a significant section of the British public still believes in the late 1990s that they would be better off under the strident, autocratic style of Margaret Thatcher than under the more conciliatory approach of John Major. While there is no doubt of the impact of Margaret Thatcher's premiership during the 1980s, there *is* doubt about whether her style would be relevant in the changed circumstances of the late 1990s. Despite the inevitable movement towards more empowerment, the customer-driven environment and a rapidly changing global market, people still want to be led by an individual.

It is evident from all this that the relationship between leadership and teams is a complex one. There appear to be forces working against each other. On the one hand is the movement towards a more democratic/empowered approach and on the other is the stubborn insistence on staying with the solo leader – all within an environment of chaotic change. It is this chaos which is causing the dilemma. Organizations are not prepared to invest more in teams, at the expense of leaders, unless they are convinced it will work. After all, an ad hoc team will not necessarily produce a better result than individuals working separately. This will only happen if the team is properly trained – and that takes money and time.

The remainder of this chapter will address this dilemma and focus on the team circle in Adair's model (see p. 15) in order to analyse the implications for teamwork in the future, and to propose possible solutions to overcome this problem.

The Impact of Change

The rate of change is so fast now that it is difficult to remember what life was like before. In effect it was the world recession at the beginning of the 1990s that finally put paid to 'the good old days', although those days were dying long before then. They were characterized by hierarchies consisting of several layers of management (British Telecom had 14 in 1991), by autocratic leadership, restricted information and a slow decision-making process, the latter largely due to the 'solo leader' approach which required a decision from 'the boss' on most issues. Inevitably, this wasted a considerable amount of time and led to a good deal of frustration throughout organizations. Sadly, this approach still exists today in thousands of establishments in both the public and the private sectors, right across the world. They are easy to identify: they are typified by chief executives who never have enough time, who do most things themselves because 'no one else can do it better', who constantly interfere with the work of their subordinates and who are unwilling to share information.

Another reason for the slow decision making in the past was that there was no requirement to make decisions as quickly as today because the resources to do so did not exist. It is only the emergence of sophisticated computer systems linked to mass communications which has made this possible. The sheer impact of such technology is difficult to recall now, but one of the authors has a vivid memory of the introduction of new systems to the Ministry of Defence in London during the Falklands War in 1982. It revolutionized the working methods in that building in days, and enabled the staff to cope with the dramatic increase in workload associated with the nation prosecuting a war for the first time since the Suez crisis, 26 years earlier.

It must also be remembered that decision making was not considered to be slow in the pre-computer age: people thought they were working as fast as they could, which indeed they were. It is also easy to overlook the advantages of the old style of leadership. The working environment tended to be well ordered with everyone clear about their role and position in the organization. There tended to be clear direction from the top emanating from a 'single voice' (usually, quite literally) and, although it might have taken time, when decisions were taken (usually after reasoned consideration) they were implemented logically over a period of time. What a change from today!

The New Environment

The new environment is one of bewildering change. This is as true of politics, business, education and medicine as it is of social issues, leisure, travel and sport. The rate of change is hectic. It has accelerated as a result of technological advances which are now enabling people to achieve ambitions that have challenged the human race for centuries. For example, achievements in the mid-1990s have included the building of the Channel Tunnel (an extraordinary engineering feat), the link-up in space between the American shuttle and the Russian space station, and astonishing medical successes which have made it possible to extend significantly the life span of the human race.

These achievements, combined with the promise (or threat) of a future embracing a world of virtual reality, a cashless society and a life increasingly dominated by the Internet, have given a spur to our imagination. We can see that it really is possible for us to do the things which we thought were beyond our grasp only a few years ago – if we want to. There is a choice, and it is at the heart of our attitude to change. This perplexity has been exacerbated by the perception of inefficiency of governments at both national and local levels, and the apparent failure of society to resolve the fundamental issues which affect our daily lives. For instance, we can build a tunnel under the Channel, but are unable to prevent the trains that use it from breaking down. The political frustration is best exemplified by the tragic war in the former Yugoslavia where events slipped back to a world of human misery, wanton destruction, ethnic cleansing and a refugee problem of tragic proportions, similar to Europe in the 1940s. Despite all the technological advances of the modern world, diplomats, politicians and soldiers deployed under the humanitarian banner of the UN struggled, powerless, for more than three years to resolve this human tragedy.

Similarly, opposing forces have operated against each other in the wake of the world recession as the old established order has struggled to adjust to the modern world, and the new order has pressed for more radical reforms. Although these forces have usually been reflected by different generations, this is not always the case. Indeed, there are many examples of radicalism amongst the over-fifties and cautious conservatism amongst the young. It is all a matter of attitude.

Whatever its composition, the old established order has been challenged on all fronts by change and this has exerted fundamental influences on organisations. The drive for efficiency and quality, the economic realities and the increasing competitiveness in the world markets have forced organizations to reduce drastically the core workforce and cut levels of management to unprecedented levels. British Telecom, Britain's biggest company, had a staff of 240 000 in 1990. By 1993, this was down to 170 000 – and the target is 115 000 by 1997. Similarly, the 14 levels of management were reduced to seven by 1993. But it is not just the downsizing which has affected companies, it is also the need to react faster and more effectively to new markets; and also the requirement to face fresh challenges not even perceived a few years ago.

This has resulted in an exciting era which has provided the stimulus for creativity, bright ideas and imaginative projects. One has only to listen to the young enthusiastic computer literates to realize what the present is to them: it is the future – now. But it is also the era of the lost. There are thousands of people who have no comprehension of this new dawn, no confidence in their ability to cope. Many of these have been made redundant and condemned to continuous unemployment. Even for those who remain in work, life is not straightforward since they are desperate to keep their jobs. As a result, they do what is asked of them, work harder and for longer hours to compensate for the reduction in the workforce, only thankful to still be in employment. No wonder that stress levels in Britain are the highest they have ever been. Recent studies by government departments in the UK indicate that the country is losing in the order of one hundred million working days a year with associated costs of up to £10 billion per annum – ie over £1500 a year for every member of the British workforce (Cooper *et al.*, 1991).

In many organizations the management of change has just 'happened'. There has been no planned strategy through this age of uncertainty. There has been little support, not much direction and, worst of all, no training. In many companies, the relationship between leadership and teams simply does not exist. As a result, the gap between the organizations which have adapted successfully to change and those which have not, is getting wider and wider.

Recipe for Success

The key to success for team leadership lies in the shift from old-fashioned management to new-style leadership. It is founded on the concept of the 'soft issues' and is all about the relationship between the leader and the team. We now consider the key elements required to enable a team to meet the challenges of the future.

Trust and Openness

No team will succeed if there are barriers between any of the members. The way to overcome this is by building an atmosphere of trust and openness. This has to be based on the *values* and *example* of the leadership. There are no half-measures in this since it is not possible to be 'partially' open. Total trust, based on sound values, provides the foundation for the culture of the team. This is reinforced by the personal example of the leadership. Leaders can often mislead their superiors, but they cannot disguise their true worth from their team members. Leaders who do not do what they say are always exposed by their team members in the end. Lack of *integrity* often provides the barrier to change.

Clear Direction

Teams need to be clear about where they are going. This should be based on a *shared vision* and *agreed goals*. The old-style management often provided clear direction, but this was frequently imposed. Team members need to be involved with the decision-making process right from the beginning: only then will they become stake holders. Furthermore, a sense of ownership from the outset will ensure that there is no subsequent confusion.

Open Communications

Shared information is crucial to team effectiveness and most problems in teams can be traced to a breakdown in communications. Sometimes this is deliberate (as when an individual retains information in order to keep power) or it may be accidental. Whatever the reason, teams need to ensure that communications are kept open at all times. This is not easy to achieve and it requires a continual emphasis, especially a conscious effort to listen. Open communication is essential for real empowerment.

Team Competence

The competence of a team is based on the most effective use of the strengths of its members, and an understanding of their weaknesses, so that these can be compensated. This, in turn, leads to flexibility and an ability to rise to challenges and, as the team matures, to seek further challenges. This maturity takes time to develop and is based on learning from experience, on honest reviews of progress and on the confidence gained from the team achieving success. The very best teams are those which are self-motivated, creative, take crises in their stride, have a telepathic understanding and build on their experience. A team with all these ingredients will contain members who are totally fulfilled and, above all else, enjoy their work. Indeed, the best teams do not consider what they do as being 'work' at all.

Can this level of teamwork be achieved by ordinary people? The answer is a firm 'Yes'. The measures to achieve this will be addressed shortly, but first, let us consider some examples of successful teams which follow the principles just outlined. It is important to emphasize that the examples are drawn from across the spectrum of both the private and the public sectors. The relevance of this is that the recipe for success is applicable for any team, be it a sports team, a management board, a work shift, a military unit or an orchestra. The characteristics are transferable across the full range of disciplines.

Sport provides some excellent evidence of world-class teams and this provides good case studies because achievements are measurable and self-evident: there is no dispute about a team which has won a world championship. Some teams, however, only achieve this status for a short period. The ones in which we are interested are those which have sustained their position at the top for a long period, those that are truly world class. Such teams include the West Indies cricket team of the 1970s and 1980s, McLaren and Williams Formula 1 racing teams, the San Francisco 49ers and, from Rugby Union, the All Blacks.

David Kirk (captain of the All Black World Cup champions in 1987) focused on five qualities of greatness: vision, ability, divine discontent, discipline and politics. His interpretation of two of the qualities are revealing. 'Divine discontent' he defines as 'an attitude to learning and growth that is never satisfied with past achievements but is always searching for new challenges' (Kirk, 1992). This self-critical approach is a characteristic of top teams and, for instance, is a crucial aspect in the training of Royal Marine Commandos. The other interesting interpretation is 'politics', which he views as the management of interpersonal relationships in a team.

All of his qualities would sit well with organizations in both the private and public sectors. The measure of the All Blacks' achievement is that they were acknowledged as the best in the world some five years before the inaugural World Cup in 1987, and have remained 'the team to beat' ever since. Recent successes have included reaching the World Cup Final in 1995, and winning the Southern Hemisphere Tri-Nations Competition in 1996. Their demolition of England in the first twenty minutes of the semi-final of the 1995 World Cup illustrated what Kirk means by vision: 'the world class teams I played with had a vision ... of moving the playing of rugby union on to a higher plane. We were simply trying to play the game better than any team had ever played it before.' That All Blacks' performance against England (who were a very good team and amongst the favourites) eight years after their inaugural win underlines the essential constant improvement of real world-class teams.

Interestingly, the manager of the England team that afternoon was Jack Rowell. At that time he had only been in the post for a year and, although he had led England to winning the Five Nations Championship (England, Scotland, Ireland, Wales and France) in his first season, he recognized that he had insufficient time to build a truly world-class side. He was appointed to England as a result of his achievements with Bath (which *was* a world class rugby club). Under his guidance, they won the Pilkington Cup (the England Rugby Cup knockout competition) eight times during the period 1984–94 and the Courage Clubs League championship title five times in the first seven years of its existence. Rowell, a successful businessman as the chief executive of Golden Wonder Crisps, applied his business management principles to Bath and subsequently to England. He was a director of a company that was acquired by Dalgety Plc. On acquisition, he was made chief executive of Golden Wonder, a company that was underperforming at that time. He turned it round to such an extent that it became the prize of the group. His philosophy, in business and rugby, is based on empowerment. He believes that, if you choose the right people, and then trust them, they will respond. He welcomes challenge from within his teams; indeed, he encourages it – and then challenges people to improve. He looks for strong individuals who have the confidence to express themselves and who will strive for continuous improvement. Rowell is critically aware of the time it takes to develop a world-class team and it will be intriguing to see whether he can achieve at the international level what he has managed with Bath Rugby Club and Golden Wonder Crisps. What is already clear from this example is the interrelationship between the team skills of business and sport.

The military is another field which has a strong emphasis on teamwork. Despite the overt hierarchy, there is a strong bond across the ranks based on mutual respect, shared discomfort and danger, and reliance on the professional competence of individuals. This is all part of the ethos of the military and is forged right at the beginning, during training. This is nowhere more evident than in the Royal Marines. Officers and recruits train side-by-side and are required to undergo the same tests in order to achieve the coveted green beret. These tests include, amongst other things, an arduous endurance course, an assault course (known as the Tarzan Assault Course because the first part requires individuals to negotiate rope obstacles high in the trees), a nine-mile speed march and 30 miles across Dartmoor. Naturally, as the Commando tests are designed to prepare people for war, everyone undertakes these evolutions wearing full battle order (which weighs some 30lb – when it is dry) and carrying a rifle. The course has been described as one that would test an Olympic athlete, even in ordinary running clothing and footwear.

The philosophy behind the Royal Marine training is based on teamwork: the need to rely implicitly on one's comrades. No individual will get through the course on his own. At some stage, everyone will face their own Everest and have to turn to the group to help them through. Such training enables ordinary individuals to overcome challenges they had previously thought impossible. It also teaches them to trust their instructors who, having led by example, then stand back, motivate and encourage. The standards are high and nobody is permitted to slip through the net. However, within reason, there is latitude over the number of attempts permitted at the various tests. This acknowledges that individuals vary in their maturity and in the time it takes to reach peak fitness. Success, when it comes, is celebrated by the instructors and trainees alike.

The bonding of such training lasts for life. It is a special club where all members have been tested against the same standards and learned to rely on each other completely. It is founded on resilience and it breeds determination, flexibility, trust, openness, tolerance and appreciation of the strengths of others – and of one's own weaknesses.

The examples of good teamwork from business and industry embrace some of the best known names in commerce. These include the Japanese firms of Sony, Toyota, Nissan and Honda, all renowned for their quality products. The American firms which have focused on teamwork include Hewlett Packard, General Electric, AT&T, Levi Strauss, Motorola and W.L. Gore. From Britain, such a roll-call would include Virgin, The Body Shop, Rolls-Royce and Asda. To this list of household names can be added hundreds of smaller companies who have realized the strength of open communications and empowerment.

One such company is Frederick Theak, a shirt and neckwear manufacturer of high international reputation which has concentrated on the quality end of the market. The company was established in London in 1885 and relocated to Taunton in the West Country during the Second World War. An amicable take-over of the Somerset Manufacturing Company in 1966, and the addition of another shirt-making business (Day Foley of Ilminster) in 1985, resulted in the current situation of a two-site company, employing 187 people with a turnover of £4.6 million. The recession in the early 1990s hit Theak's as hard as anyone else. Increasingly aware of the competition, managing director Nigel Barker realized that in order to survive he needed to establish a niche market and, to help him achieve this, he decided to involve people more in the business. The resulting empowerment and energetic marketing resulted in a 10 per cent increase in exports in just six months in 1995. He knows that he still has a lot more to do but the release of the potential of his workforce has already enabled him to make considerable progress which has had an impact on the bottom line. Significantly, he sets the example from the top and, like so many in his position, he is working much longer hours than in the 1980s. But setting an example to a team requires more than that. In order to be effective it needs to be measurable. Barker has set himself the target of answering every fax within 12 hours – six if possible. With customers all round the world, this sets a standard of quality and provides a great example to his people (interview, 30 June 1995).

This move to empowerment is one that has spread worldwide and it is dynamic. With its origins in Deming's focus on quality in the 1950s which so influenced the Japanese, it has spread from Asia to infiltrate the Americas and Europe. Interestingly, although the principles are the same, the successful organizations are those which have adapted them to their own national culture rather than slavishly following the imported model (thus reinforcing Fons Trompenaars' impressive research into culture – Trompenaars, 1993).

One of the best examples of this transformation is the adaptation of Japanese work practices amongst the British workforce of such companies as Nissan, Honda and Toshiba. This also occurred in Anglo-Japanese joint venture between Rover and Honda in the late 1980s and early 1990s. Acceptance of the national culture is important: a straightforward import of say, Japanese work practice, will not work. This has been recognized by Ricardo Semler, the successful Brazilian businessman and author of *Maverick* (1993), who, when changing his organization from a bureaucratic one to an empowered company, recognized that the Japanese system was basically paternalistic. His aim was to remove the paternalism of his family-owned company.

Another successful exponent of empowerment was Jan Carlzon, when president of Scandinavian Airlines. One of his aims at SAS was to 'create a secure working environment that fosters flexibility and innovation' (Carlzon, 1989). He saw this as an essential step on the way to full empowerment where individuals were encouraged to take responsibility for their own decisions, rather than rely on instructions from above.

Perhaps the most important development in the commercial world to date is that of self-directed work teams (SDWT). So fashionable is this movement in the United States that it comes as a surprise to learn that the origins of this concept are generally attributed to an Englishman, Eric Trist, and other members of the Tavistock Group after the Second World War. Trist was the co-author of a paper which challenged many of the assumptions of scientific management by Frederick Taylor at the beginning of the twentieth century and developed subsequently by Henry Ford (Fisher, 1993). SDWTs are the ultimate in empowerment and are characterized by:

- shared goals,
- devolved responsibility,
- shared information,
- being customer-driven,
- a multi-skilled workforce,
- a flat management structure,
- being values-based,
- being self-controlled,
- continuous improvement.

The reason this approach has become so popular is that it provides competitive advantage driven by the philosophy of a comprehensive business focus. The companies which have adopted this initiative include AT&T, Xerox, Procter & Gamble, Honeywell and Shell. In a study carried out by the National Association of Manufacturers of 1042 American factories in 1994, it was revealed that 56 per cent of them were trying out cell manufacturing (a technique whereby small teams of workers are responsible for complete produces) to some extent (*Economist*, 17 December 1994).

Another reason why SDWTs have been adopted is that flatter management structures have resulted in impractical spans of control which have overloaded individuals. Thus, although the speed of response is improved, the pressure on the individual is increased. In effect, the adoption of this system breaks down large organizations into smaller units. This enables large companies to behave like small ones. But it only works if the philosophy of empowerment is pursued fully, and for many organizations that is a step they are not prepared to take. It is these companies, the ones that are not prepared to take the risk with their people or to train them for this change, who are falling behind in an increasingly competitive world.

Developing the Team for the Future

Developing an effective team takes time, and there are no short cuts. This has always been the case, but it is even more relevant today when organizations are attempting to produce world-class teams consisting of empowered individuals. The example already outlined of Jack Rowell's attempt to develop the England rugby team into world champions in his first year underlines the need for development time. Those organizations which are not prepared to devote the resources and time to train their teams need to recognize that they will never produce world-class performance. If they are not prepared to invest, it would be better for them not to embark on the journey at all.

Having faced up to this situation and, on the basis that such an investment is considered worthwhile, let us consider the process of development. It is divided into three parts: understanding the individual, understanding the team and training the team.

Understanding the Individual

The comprehension of the individual is essential to the development of any team. This starts with understanding oneself and is based on the ideas developed in the previous chapter. As has already been explained, the behaviour and capability of an individual stems from self-image. This objective analysis can be obtained via psychometrics such as FIRO-B or the Myers-Briggs Type Indicator (MBTI) which are well proven, effective and are being used increasingly by organizations in both the public and the private sectors. In particular, these analytical systems help to reveal the hidden potential of people and enable the team to deal with, say, the brilliant individual who may have idiosyncrasies. Increasingly, competition has focused companies on the need to embrace such individuals in their culture in order to achieve a competitive edge.

With the proviso that such methods are facilitated by a trained individual, it is recommended that this is the first step in developing the team. Not only is it fascinating to discover the reason why one reacts in a certain way in a given situation, it is essential to understand oneself. This knowledge, together with the realization that everyone has strengths and weaknesses, provides the key to the necessity for teamwork – a need for complementary skills. After all, if we could do everything ourselves, there would be no requirement for a team.

Such individual analysis is best done as a team, with a facilitator explaining the process to the group and then providing feedback to each individual in turn. This helps to break down the barriers and start the bonding process, and it does need to be done. There are far too many organizations who have never been through such a process, rejecting this option through ignorance, scepticism or fear. As a result, there are millions of people who are under stress, anxious and non-effective, simply because they do not understand themselves. For those working as part of a team, which is most of us, the impact on the others is disruptive and wasteful, even more so if the leader of the group does not know his or her own strengths and weaknesses, as is evident from so many leadership roles today.

Understanding the Team

'The whole is more than the sum of the parts.' These words written by Aristotle over 2000 years ago underlie the philosophy of teamwork and also indicate that there is nothing fundamentally new about all this. The trouble is that, as life has quickened and become more complex, so we seem to have forgotten to apply common sense.

Every team is different and reflects the personalities of the individuals who are part of the group, and is dependent on members' relationships with each other, how much people contribute and participate, and whether or not there is an open atmosphere. The dynamics of a group are such that it will alter when individuals leave or join it. Such movement will require adjustment by everyone to the new relationship, just as we adjust to similar changes quite normally in our daily lives. However, these adjustments, while being adequate for normal circumstances, can prove inadequate in stressful situations which, in turn, affects the performance of the team.

In order to compensate for this it is necessary to develop a proper understanding of team dynamics. Once again, this can be accomplished with the assistance of personality profiling using such systems as the MBTI, Belbin or Team Climate Inventory (TCI). These are based on an initial questionnaire which identifies the characteristics of the individual, which can then be used to analyse human relationships or translated into the roles required in a team. This analysis should be handled by an experienced facilitator because it is probable that such an exercise will arouse considerable interest and a great number of questions, while answering queries and interpreting symptoms requires skill and experience. It is particularly important to handle sensitively some of the less attractive behaviours of individuals, since this can arouse emotions in a group situation. However, such a process is essential if a team has aspirations to become effective. There has been wariness over such 'group work' in the past and people have been put off by the perception of the weird element on the fringe of psychoanalysis. However, the use of such profiling systems as those mentioned above are in common use amongst a large number of organizations today. Another useful model is the research carried out by Margerison and McCann (1990) into the essential tasks carried out by teams. Their approach builds on the work of Meredith Belbin (1981, 1993) and incorporates an increased psychological perspective based on the 'work preferences' approach put forward by the psychologist Jung.

Carl Jung's research (1971) into personality type identified the fact that people's apparent random behaviour disguised preferences which were based on consistencies in the way they used the process of perception and judgement. The research also revealed that these consistencies helped to establish patterns which made it possible to understand an individual's needs, behaviour and motivation. This knowledge provides for a better understanding of oneself and also of other people, thus helping to forge better human relationships, especially in the workplace. Jung's research (and the subsequent development of his ideas by such people as Myers and Briggs, and Margerison and McCann) have revealed that, although an individual can carry out functions in a team, there is a natural preference for one function over another and therefore they will be more comfortable, and better, performing that one.

Quite often the above systems are used in conjunction with team-building exercises. The normal procedure is for the group to carry out a series of tasks followed by an analysis of the process. During the subsequent review, the profiles of individuals and the group are used to help interpret the behaviour during the exercise. Such a process in the hands of skilful and experienced trainers can enable a team to develop a very good understanding of itself.

Training the Team

The third part of the process is concerned with training the team. In reality, the training will already have commenced with the development of the understanding of the individual and the team. However, these parts have been separated in this chapter to emphasize that there is a proper process to developing a team which stretches over time. How long this takes and what is involves will depend on the level of the team at the start and the rate at which it matures. It also acknowledges the principle that all teams progress through four stages of development:

Forming
Storming
Norming
Performing.

The relevance of this progression is that teams are unable to move on to the next stage unless they have successfully negotiated the previous one. For instance, no team will truly be able to perform unless it has normalized its internal relations which, in turn, will have necessitated a 'storming'. This is potentially the most disruptive stage of a team's development and, as a result, many fight shy of this stage and refuse to face up to it. The important fact is that 'storming' is a normal and essential stage of maturity. Those potential teams who refuse to go through this process will not progress any further. Some of those who do find the experience so painful that they break up and disintegrate. Even those that reach the zenith of 'performing' may face a crisis at some later stage and have to drop back down the process to the 'storming' phase in order to normalize again.

This movement in team development is quite normal and emphasizes the dynamics of the process. It also explains why there are not too many real teams around. Yet this need not be the case. All that is required is:

- Determination to succeed
- Allocation of resources (including money, time and people)
- A good facilitator
- A proper training programme.

The first two points need no further explanation. The requirement for a good facilitator is an obvious requirement but many organizations have difficulty in identifying one – mainly because they are unaware of the need. The key is for the facilitator to work in partnership with the leadership to define the requirement. From this will stem the outline training programme and the timescale. It is essential to involve the leadership in this process because the commitment from the leader is vital to success. It is also important for the organization to be aware that the facilitator has the full support of the leadership. An example of this was experienced by one of the present authors when running a weekend team-building programme for a department of a national insurance company. The financial director, who was the ultimate boss of a small finance department of some 20 people, drove two hours from his home on the Saturday morning to give a five-minute opening address before returning home. The commitment he demonstrated underpinned the whole weekend. It was further cemented when he returned for the final review on the Monday morning. He also exercised empowerment and trust by not staying on longer on the Saturday morning.

The training programme should be designed to develop the team progressively over a period of time. It will commence with the analysis of individuals and the team and it should involve a team-building exercise designed to create better understanding and bond the group together. One of the important aspects of this stage is for the team to undergo an experience which is unique to them so that it bonds the individuals together. This is usually done by means of some outdoor activity but this is not essential. What is important is the team learning process (Figure 6.1).

This procedure should be adopted at each stage. The rate of progress is carefully monitored by the facilitator who should be sufficiently flexible to introduce additional evolutions if necessary to enable the team to improve on a particular aspect of their performance which may have been identified during an activity or subsequently at the review.

This team-building exercise should be reinforced at a suitable stage later on by something associated with the actual work which the team does. This could take the form of a seminar or discussion about a particular aspect of work, or it could be a case study. Whatever form it takes, it should involve the whole team. Furthermore, it must be properly prepared, with written briefs issued well in advance, and the event should be organized away from the workplace. This is crucial. Taking the team away for the day to a comfortable environment will ensure that people give their full attention to the subject in a relaxed atmosphere. This approach is conducive to quality work, reinforces the bonding and adds to the enjoyment. It is also important that the leadership participate in this 'Away Day', and it is preferable for the facilitation to be done by someone outside the team. This is because the purpose is to develop leadership and teamwork. Therefore the leader needs to operate as part of the team – not outside it.

The participation of the leadership is also essential in the final evolution, the simulation exercise. One of the best ways to hone the maturity of a team is to subject it to a simulation which reflects as near as possible the real situation of a given scenario. It may be centred on a specific incident, a

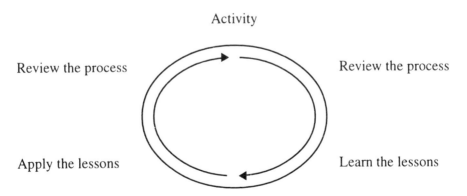

Figure 6.1   The team learning process

crisis or a series of incidents. Whatever the scenario, the key is to make it as realistic as possible through role-play, induced pressure and flexibility. In order to be successful, simulations need to be organized by people outside the team so that the individuals can operate in their own natural environment. It should also be sufficiently flexible for the organizers to be able to react to the initiatives of the players. Naturally, this requires careful preparation as well as experienced facilitators, but the results are well worth the allocation of resources. The military are particularly good at this and are able to induce such realistic pressure that on occasions 'the players' have believed themselves to be in a real war environment.

As well as the team-building exercise, the review is crucial. Above all, it is important to focus on the process and learn from the experience. It is probable that people will make mistakes. That does not matter and is, in fact, a fundamental part of the development of a team. Nobody should be blamed for mistakes, indeed, people should be encouraged to experiment and take risks. It is only by doing this that people will learn and improve.

A team-building programme such as the one described should be developed over a long period, allowing sufficient time for the team to consolidate the lessons of each stage at the workplace before progressing to the next phase. The key factor is to guide the maturity of the team so that it is able to rise to a new challenge at each step of the journey. The trick is to raise the challenge sufficiently each time so that the team actually achieves what it thought was too difficult at the beginning of that particular evolution.

The other important factor is that the facilitators should become progressively less directive, so that the proper process of empowerment is practised.

Empowerment

So far we have concentrated on the educational and training aspects of developing the team for the future. In this final section we will look at the leadership role in teamwork. It can be summed up in one word – empowerment. This has probably created more difficulty and confusion than any other aspect associated with this topic. The difficulty for many leaders and managers, at all levels, is associated with the requirement for them to step back and 'enable' other members of the team, to give them the freedom to perform. Many are not prepared to take that risk and trust their people. In addition, there is usually another problem: they are not sure what their own role is in this new environment. This is quite understandable since so many organizations are promoting empowerment (because it is the latest 'buzz' word) without any comprehension of its implications and, worst of all, without preparing their managers for their new role.

One of the problems is the hierarchical triangle, which has the leader at the apex. Even those organizations which have flattened their management structure still have a hierarchy. That is unlikely to change for, even as the workload is devolved more through teams, there will probably still be a hierarchy of teams, but one operating functionally on the episodic, ambient and strategic levels. One of the ways to understand empowerment is to move away from the traditional management triangle and invert it. Those organizations which have done this have discovered an immediate change in the relationship between the leader and the team. The emphasis changes from 'what I require from you' to 'what support do you want from me?' (*Economist*, 8 July 1995).

The inverted triangle will not be suitable for every circumstance but it serves to illustrate the change of role for the leader. Empowerment requires the leader to be a coach, a mentor, an educator and a supporter. It involves a good deal of patience, observation and encouragement and it cannot be achieved without a close relationship between the leader and the individuals in the team. It requires the leader to nurture the development of the individuals so that they grow in confidence and competence over a period of time. There can be no such timescale for this development because it will depend on the rate of progress of each individual, all of whom will mature differently. The mechanism for monitoring this development is the appraisal which should provide the opportunity each year to review the self-development programme.

The strength of empowerment is that it enables a team to develop the full potential of all its members and is thus the true descendant of Aristotle's dictum. It also puts the emphasis on 'the team' rather than 'the leader'. This, in turn, reduces the focus on personality-driven organizations led by 'hero leaders' in favour of a team culture with emphasis on the talents of everyone in the organization. In effect, everyone becomes a leader in their own way because each person takes responsibility for their own actions.

This has enormous benefit for leaders at the top of an organization because they can focus properly at the strategic level, confident that everyone around them is fulfilling their own roles competently. It also provides a natural environment for the identification of those who have the potential for the strategic level. The nurturing of these individuals and succession planning are fundamental to the continued success and progression of an organization. Sadly, this crucial element of team leadership is so often overlooked. Those who ignore this in the future are likely to jeopardize their enterprise since the speed and complexity of work in the future will demand a seamless continuation of team leadership.

Summary

In order to be world-class in future, organizations will have to be extremely flexible and able to react very quickly to an ever-changing environment. This will include a requirement for highly skilled people who can operate as part of an ad hoc project team as well as they do with their own group. It will require a flexibility by the individual to be equally comfortable working independently, remotely or on-site with their team. It also implies a growing trend towards virtual reality and computer competence.

In such an environment, it is probable that people will perform best when they operate within a culture with which they are familiar and comfortable. People are better able to face the uncertainty of the future if they are surrounded by people whom they trust to help and support them. This is why teamwork is so vital to the future of organizations and why team leadership is such an important skill to acquire. Furthermore, the longer

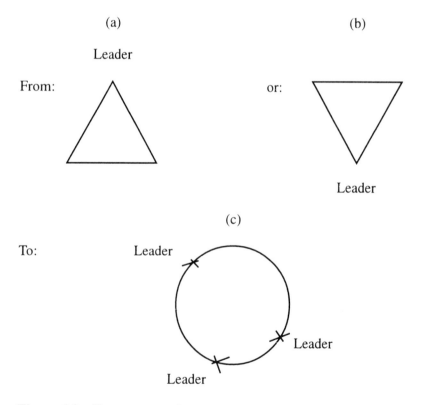

Figure 6.2   Empowerment

people stay with a good team, the more effective it becomes, and the happier they become. In order to face the challenges of tomorrow, organizations need to develop high-quality teams at all levels. The most sophisticated will operate in an atmosphere of complete trust and competence in which the leadership role moves naturally around the group, depending on the circumstances and individual skills. In effect, the hierarchy triangles will be replaced by a circle of openness and trust (see Figure 6.2). It is only in such a culture that the leader can really be part of the team the whole time.

References

Belbin, M. (1981), *Management Teams: Why They Succeed or Fail*, Oxford: Butterworth–Heinemann.

Belbin, M. (1993), *Team Roles at Work*, Oxford: Butterworth–Heinemann.

Carlzon, J. (1989), *Moments of Truth*, New York: Harper Collins.,

Cooper, C.L., Cooper, R.D. and Eaker, L.H. (1991), *Living with Stress*, Harmondsworth: Penguin.

Fisher, K. (1993), *Leading Self-Directed Work Teams*, New York: McGraw-Hill.

Jung, C.G. (1971), *Psychological Types, Bollingen Series XX The Collected Works of C.G. Jung*, Vol. 6, Princeton: Princeton University Press.

Kirk, D. (1992), 'World-class Teams', *The McKinsey Quarterly*, no. 4.

Margerison, C. and McCann, D. (1990), *Team Management*, London: Mercury Books.

Semler, R. (1993), *Maverick*, London: Century.

Trompenaars, F. (1993), *Riding the Waves of Culture*, London: Economist Books.

7   Leadership Competencies

In the last chapter we looked at the ingredients that make for a successful team. These are naturally related to the competencies required for leadership, which is the focus of this chapter. What do we mean when we talk of 'competencies' with regard to leadership? *Chambers Dictionary* definition includes the words 'sufficient; capable'. This qualification is echoed in the world of sport. When John Barclay (Manager of the England cricket touring team to Zimbabwe and New Zealand in 1996/97 and former Captain of Sussex) was asked how good a player a cricket captain should be, he replied 'good enough'.

The dictionary definition and Barclay's response are significant. They both imply that leaders do not necessarily have to be 'the best' at everything – but they should be capable of leadership. The recognition that leaders do not have to be good at everything is important in three regards. First, it reinforces the dependency that leaders have on the others in the team. Second, it argues against 'hero leaders' and thus removes the perception of leadership as an unobtainable status for the majority. Third, it fits the changing world of increasing complexity, flatter structures, remote management and virtual reality where leadership is becoming more and more a matter of shaping the energies of other specialists in the team.

There is a natural overlap between the competencies required for leadership and for management, and such a list can be extensive. It is therefore intended to focus on seven broad requirements for leadership and analyse their meaning and use in practical terms. This process embraces the three levels of leadership (episodic, ambient and strategic) as well as the future work environment of the new millennium. It will be seen that, although there may be new interpretations, much of what follows is familiar. This should be reassuring because it reinforces the view that there is nothing magical about leadership. It is all about applied common sense.

Setting Direction

John Adair believes that leadership is about a sense of direction. In stating this, he has put his finger on the nerve of leadership which is both essential and difficult. If one analyses those organizations which appear to be failing or who have apparently lost their way, the fault can usually be found to be either a breakdown in communications or a lack of direction; quite often, it is a case of both!

Setting direction involves two aspects. The first is having a clear idea of where to go, and the second is the management of how to get there (Figure 7.1). It is this combination which provides the problem because the first part requires imagination and creativity whereas the second involves good organization. It is rare to find these two qualities invested in one person, hence the difficulty if the leadership responsibility is vested in one individual.

Let us consider the 'where to go' first. For many people, this is a very difficult skill. Most of us are in positions where we are required to react to situations. In most circumstances this is a comfortable environment which involves familiar relationships and well tried procedures and is fundamentally about the management process. But leadership should be proactive and, increasingly, it is concerned with creativity. In the environment of continual change, the requirement for leadership today is to chart the way ahead, constantly challenging the unknown. Essentially this is to do with vision.

Vision lies at the heart of leadership and yet it is open to considerable misunderstanding, and some suspicion. There is a view that vision is only obtainable by a few talented individuals who possess some special insight. Indeed, it is this perception that helps to extend the myth that leaders are

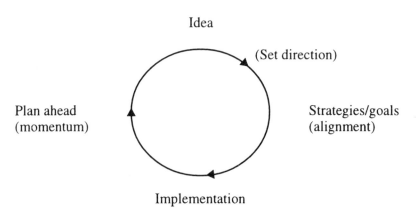

Figure 7.1   Setting direction

born, not made. In the context of leadership, vision is a picture of a desirable ambition for the team. For example, at the strategic level it could be to provide a mobile phone for every adult in the country whereas, at the episodic level it might be to provide a perfect working relationship for a night shift in a factory. Vision requires creativity and foresight and is an essential first step in setting direction.

But vision on its own is not sufficient. In order for it to be effective, the second part of this competence is required: managing the process of 'getting there'. This is about turning the ideas into reality and involves the management process of defining strategies and goals, and setting objectives. But it is more than that. In order to make this transition it is necessary to involve the people in the team who will actually effect change. This means that they have to be personally involved in the creative ideas – ideally, they should be involved in creating the vision itself. Without this 'ownership' it will be difficult to get the team's full commitment. This involvement is very much a leadership issue.

Because it is rare for one individual to be sufficiently talented to do all this on their own, increasingly, organizations are turning to the combined talents of the individuals within a team to meet and cope with the complexities of work. It follows that the involvement of the team in shaping the vision at the beginning will not only ensure commitment but will also help the alignment to ensure that the chosen direction for the group is maintained. This will also help if the team has to change direction in response to new circumstances. Such flexibility is essential if organizations are to meet the challenges of the future.

Setting an Example

The example provided by leaders is crucial to the relationship with their teams. Their behaviour, the way they treat people, their reaction in a crisis, their attitude to ethical matters are all observed closely by followers. The subsequent commitment will depend significantly on the judgement of that observation although the significance will vary, depending on the nature and the nationality of the organization (for instance, there will be a less obvious relationship in a paternalistic culture than in one that is democratic).

Example is usually viewed in the context of the relationship between the leader and subordinates. This is important because, although an individual in a leadership role may be able to hide their real personality from their superiors, and even their peers, they will not be able to fool their subordinates. This is one of the reasons why skilful strategic leaders spend much of their time at shop floor level in order to discover whether they have a true perspective about the leaders operative at the ambient level. They can only obtain the full picture by talking to followers.

Essentially, example is bedded in the beliefs and values of an individual, which were discussed in Chapter 5. These are the foundations of a person's behaviour which, in turn, relates to their integrity. It is important for an individual to clarify these issues in their own mind before embarking on the leadership journey because their integrity will be tested constantly. Many leaders have looked in the mirror and not liked what they saw; far better to do this before starting the journey in order to find out whether the beliefs and values really are substantial.

The importance of this is associated with the openness required to gain the trust of followers. Without this there will never be a proper relationship and, as more and more organizations are discovering, without that trust it is impossible to realize the full potential of everyone in an organization. This is becoming increasingly relevant in the environment of rapid change and yet some leaders have been slow to realize the impact of personal example. For instance, there is the issue of pay for top executives. In the mid 1990s, there has been increasing pressure on chief executives in the UK to take pay cuts or have a wages freeze, against the background of employees who are being made redundant or forced to accept annual pay rises linked only to inflation. The pressure on senior executives has been relentless, from the House of Commons Select Committee, the Cadbury Committee, the Director General of the Confederation of British Industry and, increasingly, from the public. The longer such leaders resist this pressure, the greater they risk losing the confidence of their employees, and without that confidence they will not be able to make the changes needed to sustain the continual improvement so necessary for the future. A senior executive earning over £150 000 who accepts a 20 per cent pay rise is not setting a good example to an employee on £15 000 with only a 3 per cent rise.

Maybe the reluctance to demonstrate the required restraint is due to the fact that senior executives do not see an immediate disadvantage to their not doing so. This reflects the short-term approach adopted by so many organizations and it is likely to be increasingly exposed in the future, as the importance of being able to inspire people to achieve more and more becomes a key factor. Essentially, the behaviour of some top executives is preventing them from making the necessary changes for the future because their people are not fully behind them.

The example of the leader helps to establish and reinforce the culture of an organization. Leaders who are open, enthusiastic and realistic and who enjoy their work will be rewarded by a reciprocal reaction from their people. One of the pleasing characteristics about the human race is the need for role models. Such people can be 'leaders for bad' (such as Hitler or Mussolini) or they can be 'leaders for good' (Gandhi or Churchill). Reassuringly, the constant hunger for role models continues to be met.

These role models are important in the development of aspiring leaders because they help them to identify those aspects of personal example which make a difference in the relationship with their followers. Role models also exemplify *the* most important aspect of leadership example: they do what they say. People respect and follow leaders whose behaviour mirrors their words; they have no respect for leaders who say one thing and do another. Eventually, they stop following them.

Communication

Once it is clear which direction to take, this needs to be communicated to everyone. Communication is a key skill for leaders at all levels. The problem is that, although this is well understood, it is the most frequent reason cited for failure. How often have we heard people say, *'The leadership is out of touch ... they don't tell us what is going on ... they might know where they are going but we don't ... they don't listen'*.

The trouble with communication is that it is as natural as breathing so we tend not to concentrate on it. Leaders need to concentrate on the effectiveness of communication and it all starts with listening – active listening. Most people's concentration span is limited, with the result that they do not assimilate all that they hear. This was well summed up by a lorry driver from a major British company who, when asked by one of the authors whether his management listened replied: *'They listen all right – but they don't hear!'* Listening properly to what people say is the first step in the communication process. This is followed by clarifying any queries so that everyone is quite clear about what has been said. Learning to ask the right questions is also part of this process. This is especially important at the strategic level so that for instance, information can be gleaned from specialist areas which help to fit the pieces to the jigsaw before a decision can be made. Margaret Thatcher was particularly good at asking the right questions during the Falklands War when she was being briefed by military specialists. She then used this specialist knowledge to help formulate the strategic plans.

Another key skill for the leader is to communicate to others simply and effectively so that they understand what is being said and what they are required to do, and then to check this subsequently to *ensure* that people understand the message. One of the main problems with communication is that people assume that others understand what they have said when, in reality, they put another interpretation on it and end up by doing something entirely different from what was required. This can be very frustrating and in the worst case can end up with people going in the wrong direction. The best communicators are those who do so simply and effectively in order to avoid misunderstandings. The military are particularly good at this, but then, they have to be: they have learnt through bitter experience that procedures are essential in order to maintain clear communications through the chaos of battle. As the civilian world becomes more chaotic, perhaps it will adopt similar simple procedures.

The aspects discussed so far are applicable at all levels of management. The last part of this section concentrates on the strategic level because communications at the top of an institution can be particularly difficult and there are some skills which leaders can use to advantage. The first is to ensure that the vision is reinforced at every opportunity. Whether talking at the board or the shop floor level, giving speeches or talking to the Press, every opportunity should be taken to define the direction in which the organization is going. It is this combination of clear direction reinforced by constant communication which produces the alignment so essential for success.

The next point is the importance of a strategic leader getting out of the office a great deal of the time, not only to see what is happening throughout the organization, but also to listen to people – and to talk to them. Most effective top leaders are away from their head office two days a week. Although this imposes a considerable extra workload on them, they do this because they know it is an essential part of leadership, and also because, invariably, they pick up good ideas from listening to their workforce.

This leads on to the last point. By spending time with different departments, a chief executive will often become aware of embryonic ideas from Department A which may be of value to Department B. However, B does not know this because A is still at the experimental stage, or is unaware of the significance of what it is doing. In these circumstances it is usually only the chief executive who is alive to the possibilities because he is the one person bridging the gap at the strategic level – that is his function. He therefore becomes a 'communication agent' by passing on ideas from one department to another.

All these aspects of communication are straightforward and can be applied to any organization. All it needs is for the process to be started by the 90 per cent of companies who are not doing it, so that they can close the gap on the 10 per cent who are!

Alignment

Clear direction, communications and personal example are essential for the fourth competence, alignment. This is difficult to achieve, and impossible without first accomplishing the other three. Before the leadership can even attempt to align people in the organization, they have to be absolutely clear about the direction in which they are going, satisfied that the communications are open, allowing a free flow of information both ways, and confident that the followers are convinced by their integrity. Alignment involves both the unification of the individuals within the team and the fusion of the activities of the team as a whole.

Let us first consider the unification of individuals. A non-aligned team will consist of energies being dissipated in a number of directions as a result of such factors as lack of direction, little coordination, internal politics and poor morale. This has already been referred to in Chapter 3 and such a situation leads to the example shown in Figure 7.2, with the organization making little progress in the intended direction.

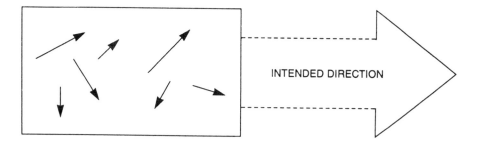

Figure 7.2 Non-aligned team

One of the most important roles of leadership is to reduce the wasted energies and align them to focus on the intended direction, as in Figure 7.3. This is best achieved by well-organized management of the process, straightforward and effective coordination, open communications and endless patience. This last point is particularly associated with internal politics which is probably the biggest cause of wasted energy. By their very nature, most people like to gossip. This is normally manipulated by a few individuals who can influence the tone of the discussion. Many a company's good intentions have been thwarted by the 'talk in the office'. It is an important role of leadership to reinforce their mission by constantly emphasizing this at every opportunity, by involving people in decision making, by welcoming their ideas and by countering false rumour and correcting inaccuracies. This is time-consuming and energy-sapping, but it is essential if the leadership is to get followers aligned with their direction.

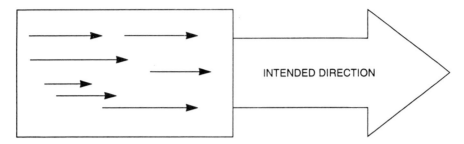

Figure 7.3   Aligned team

Once this has been achieved, the emphasis can switch to the second aspect of alignment, that of the fusion of the activities of the team as a whole. This involves a three-part process:

Clear direction
Communication
Empowerment.

The need for clear direction has already been discussed but, in this context, it is important to recognize that this may take some time to resolve. Once again, the leadership needs patience to be satisfied about the direction before communicating it throughout the organization. The second stage is crucial. Every opportunity should be taken to reinforce the strategy via all relevant means of communication. The aim is to ensure that everyone understands the direction in which the organization is going and what their part will be in achieving the aim.

The second stage may take some time, but, once the leadership is confident that all their people understand their role, they are ready to move on to the final part of the process, which is empowerment. This is the real test of alignment and it requires self-discipline by the leadership, to stand back, delegate and trust their people to get on with their jobs. After all, they are the experts in their particular field and, provided they are clear about the aim, they have the ability to achieve their particular objective as part of the goal.

Properly aligned organizations tend to succeed well above their expectations because the people at the sharp end have the confidence to use their initiative and take decisions on the spot, certain that they will be supported by the leadership. Of great importance is alignment at the strategic level. The three phases need to be underpinned by constant planning ahead so that change is managed continually. By doing this, leadership is able to be constantly proactive and relate creativity to the management process.

Bringing the Best out of People

For years, organizations have been saying that people are their most important asset. For some organizations this was a genuine statement, for others it was not. The difficulty in the past has been to find out who was telling the truth! However, this dilemma will be easier to unravel in the future because those organizations who really value their people are likely to be the ones that prosper – and the evidence will show 'on the bottom line'.

Organizations are realizing at last that, in an increasingly competitive world, it really *is* people who make the difference. That is why being able to bring the best out of people is such an important leadership competence. This is naturally related to personal example and involves such characteristics as motivation, inspiration, encouragement, trust and empowerment. The aim is to create the right atmosphere and provide the opportunity for individuals to realize their full potential. It is rather like an iceberg with only 30 per cent of its mass showing above the surface, and 70 per cent hidden below the water as shown in Figure 7.4. The requirement is to develop that hidden potential.

Because this skill is so all-embracing, it is a difficult one to master. There are many experienced senior executives who know they should be doing this and find it difficult to achieve. It requires careful thought and personal commitment to develop people, and it involves considerable time and energy. In a busy life, with increasing pressures at the higher level, many senior executives are not prepared to devote the time to do this. Some say they do not have the time, but in private will admit that they do not know how to tackle the problem.

The right personal example is the genesis of the process. A high level of integrity sets the standard and provides the model for the followers. However, this alone is insufficient. In order for a leader to be effective, a certain empathy is required. A leader who encourages people, gives praise where it

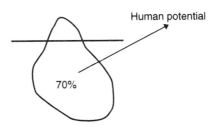

Figure 7.4   Human potential

is due, and who respects individuals will attract a response from them, thus opening the dialogue. The manner of this communication is very important. It should be open, so that an easy relationship is established in order for the leader to develop the potential of the follower. Many leaders establish the dialogue but keep it at a parent–child relationship level or, worse still, are so dominant that their people are too frightened to challenge them.

Challenge and the use of empowerment constitute the key function in the development of people. Once a good relationship has been established and the leader has got to know his people really well, the next stage is to coach them for their first challenge, and then encourage them to achieve it. The crucial factors are that each challenge should be adjusted to individual development (since everyone matures at a different rate) and that, after coaching, individuals should be left to achieve on their own. The risk is that they may fail, but that failure then becomes a learning tool which is discussed in the subsequent review. This cycle of coach–challenge–empowerment–review is repeated at regular intervals and progress is made by raising the challenge as the individual grows in confidence.

Such a process will not only develop the potential of everyone but it will also help to reveal those individuals who have the ability to go to the top of the organization. One of the important roles of leadership is to identify and develop successors. This is healthy for the company and, perhaps somewhat surprisingly, it can be rejuvenating for the managing director as well. A good example of the refreshing atmosphere resulting from an open approach to succession planning is the case of Vapormatic (an international company based at Exeter who specialize in agricultural machinery, with outlets as far afield as Canada, The United States, Australia, New Zealand and Zimbabwe). Their unofficial slogan is Project 2003, because that is the year the managing director is due to retire. The MD has promoted the idea, both to provide a target for ambitious sales and profits and also to allow plenty of time for a suitable successor to be groomed to succeed him. The management are benefiting immensely from this open approach.

It is becoming evident that the high pressure of work at the top level is taking its toll an increasing number of leaders at the head of organizations. A leader who has exceeded his 'sell by date' can become a real liability. In many cases an individual can stay on too long, either because he or she does not want to release power, or because there is no obvious successor, or for both reasons. Succession is a leadership responsibility and it is also a natural result of a policy of bringing the best out of people.

The other natural development of such a policy is teamwork, which has already been discussed in detail. The competencies identified for developing teamwork parallel many of those raised in this section, thus highlighting the holistic approach required for leadership development.

The Leader as Change Agent

Whenever a new leader is appointed there is an anticipation that, sooner or later, there will be changes. It may be that an individual is appointed with a specific remit to make changes, or changes may occur as a result of someone looking at the situation afresh. Either way, leadership and change are synonymous and it is one of the characteristics that separates leadership from management.

It is relatively easy for a new leader to bring in changes early in an appointment because it is expected and because of his different perspective. Indeed, the danger here is not to be seen to be making change for the sake of change. It is much more difficult for a leader to be a change agent once he has become well established, especially after several years in office. It requires enormous energy and resilience to start the necessary impetus at the beginning of the change process.

The requirement for leaders to rise to this challenge has never been greater because of the speed of change which we are now experiencing. It is not sufficient to be reactive; on the contrary, it is essential to be proactive, and this requires an approach which only a few have adopted. The first step is to challenge the status quo. What is required is a vigorous investigation into why things are done the way they are; this should involve an honest and objective appraisal. If the process stands up to the investigation, leave well alone. If not, consider what changes need to be made. This culture of challenge should be developed throughout the organization and the momentum should be maintained by a procedure of constant reviews so that it becomes a natural and continuous process.

This is very much part of TQM, but the extra ingredient is the role of leadership. It is associated with maintaining the momentum of change, and that is linked with the sigmoid curve (see Figure 7.5) so well explained by Charles Handy (1994). This S-shaped curve represents the life cycle of an

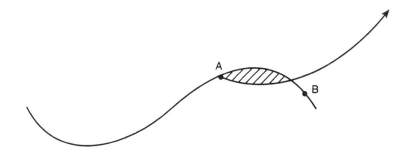

Figure 7.5 The Sigmoid curve

individual or an organization which, inevitably, waxes and then wanes. The key is to start the second curve (at Point A) before the peak and thus use the latent energy of experience from the old curve while still at the experimental stage.

There are two parts of the change process: what to change and how to change. The first part is the difficult one and involves creativity, vision and a clear sense of direction associated with strategic thinking. The second part is about implementation, but it is also linked to strategy because of the timing necessary. This is where the Sigmoid curve becomes such a useful model. Get the timing right and you can use the down curve at the beginning of the new process (when you are still learning – at Point A) while you are below the crest of the old process. Get the timing wrong (Point B) and you may never recover the lost ground.

Above all, being a change agent involves a flexible approach and being prepared to take risks – just what is required by leaders in any sphere. It also carries with it the responsibility for encouraging and coaching people to meet the challenge of change. Approached in the right way, most people will respond well to such leadership and the results usually provide a fitting regard for all the effort. However, there will be some people who do not respond to this and who are unable to change. It may be that they have other priorities or are unwilling to take the step for some reason or other. In such circumstances it is important that they do not remain part of the team. Not only is it important from their viewpoint, because they will not be happy in such an environment, but it is also important for the rest of the team who will not want their progress slowed down. Those who will not change should be treated with compassion and understanding when they leave the organization, but leave it they must. This is one of the least pleasant, but necessary, responsibilities of leadership.

Providing Decision in a Crisis and on the Ambiguous

One of the concepts most associated with leadership is that of being decisive in a crisis. Indeed, the linkage is so strong that there is a perception that this is the main purpose of leadership, resulting in the stereotype of the tough, focused, macho and decisive leader. There are many examples of such leaders today, mainly at the lower level in the military and the emergency services, where they are frequently required to make quick decisions. In such circumstances the requirements of the job almost dictate the need for a 'crisis leader', but it would be wrong to assume that such leaders are born to the job; they are not. Those who provide good leadership in such crises are able to do so because of their training.

Both the military and the emergency services recruit from the same pool as business, the service industries and the public sector. They are all looking for similar qualities (such as commitment, effective intellect and professional attitude) and therefore, at the beginning, there is little difference between their people other than the personal decision to opt for a particular job. Nowadays, you are just as likely to find someone with a master's degree in the police as in the research department of a major company. However, once they have joined their respective organization, they will undergo the training tailored to the specific requirement. As a result, the emergency services and the military prepare their people for crisis management so thoroughly that it becomes second nature. This becomes part of their culture because it is an obvious requirement.

Most other organizations do not see a requirement to deliver such training and, as there is virtually no leadership development, it is little wonder that many executives are found wanting in a crisis. However, we believe that some relevant lessons can be drawn from the example of the emergency services. Their training provides them with experience of crises through realistic simulation. Subsequently, when they are faced with a real situation, they draw upon the knowledge of that experience which gives them confidence to tackle the crisis. This knowledge and confidence also helps to develop calmness.

If we take this analogy into other areas, it suggests that knowledge is a key element in a crisis and therefore it is prudent to use appropriate expertise within the team whenever possible. Unfortunately, there are too many occasions when the senior executive tries to do it himself and ignores the available specialist. As regards calmness, some of us are naturally calm in a crisis, but most are not. However, the analogy suggests that, as calmness is associated with knowledge and experience, so it can be developed within a team, by using the specialist knowledge and experience and also the experience of others in the team (including the leader) who have gone through a similar situation previously.

The decision to empower others in a crisis, and when to do so, requires judgement – one of the key requirements of leadership in any circumstance. It is for this reason that the second part of the section heading has been inserted: *'providing decisions on the ambiguous.'* Leaders are called on to make a great number of decisions. However, most of these are unnecessary because they should really have been taken by the appropriate manager or team member and not referred to the leader at all. The genesis for this is the 'reference upwards' approach which has so bedevilled management throughout the world. It exists principally in hierarchies and paternalistic institutions in which no initiatives are permitted without the approval of the chief executive. Such an approach blunts initiative, wastes time and reduces the effectiveness of the senior executive because he spends too much time at the ambient level instead of at the strategic. However, if the CEO encourages people to make decisions at their appropriate level they will only come to him when there is genuine ambiguity – when they want a 'leadership' decision.

Summary

The areas of competencies outlined in this chapter provide a broad framework designed to meet the leadership requirements of a changing world. They embrace the embryonic, ambient and strategic levels and are within the reach of virtually everyone who aspires to becoming a leader. In the past, there has been a tendency for too rigid an approach to leadership which has resulted in the inexperienced and the young slavishly following what they have been taught, or learned by osmosis.

Leadership potential needs to be nurtured and inspired by good mentors who coach individuals through the flexible approach based on the seven categories discussed in this chapter. It is this flexibility which will enable them to adapt constantly to change. Despite the increasing dependence on technology, it is people who are still the key asset in any organization. As the 'head count' reduces and companies become leaner, so leadership becomes increasingly a matter of getting more effort from fewer people. That will only be achieved through a thorough understanding of how to motivate, inspire and develop people – how to release their full potential.

A Reminder of the Seven Leadership Insights

1   Setting direction
2   Setting an example
3   Effective communication
4   Creating alignment
5   Bringing the best out of people
6   Leader as a change agent
7   Decisions and action in crisis or uncertainty

Reference

Handy, C. (1994), *The Empty Raincoat*, London: Hutchinson.

8 What to Do in Preparation for Tomorrow

The key issue about leadership for the future is unlocking the enormous human potential by winning people's emotional support. When individuals are questioned about their idea of leadership and who makes an effective leader, they tend to think in terms of dominant characters who inspire confidence and then persuade others to their point of view. This results in altered follower behaviour. This model often assumes a lack of knowledge on the part of the followers, and also a lack of ability to question the leader's actions. More than anything else, the leaders of the future are going to have to justify their actions against the questioning of followers more then ever before. The reason for this is communication. People at all levels of society are better informed than they have been in the past and they have different expectations of themselves and of their leaders. In simple terms, our leaders of the future will have to be more competent, more articulate, more creative, more inspirational and more credible if they are going to win the hearts and minds of the followers.

This final chapter considers the way forward by looking at future trends in leadership and then proposes a 'blueprint' for leadership across the board, including the strategic level.

Future Trends

Let us now look at some of the trends that seem to be taking place which will have an impact on our leaders in organizations. These trends will affect everyone, whether they are a first line team leader or a chief executive. First, we consider the continuous trend of delayering and with it an increasing tendency to expect people at all levels within organizations to contribute more in the way of added value. To do this effectively, people need to be better informed of the wider issues in the organization, not just within their own area of responsibility. We have seen a shift from producer-centred products and services to customer-led products and services. Again, this raises the importance of the communication issue both inside and outside the organization. Leaders of the future will have to facilitate rather than constrict communication.

Life is now increasingly concerned with quality and therefore the key for leaders is to inspire people at all levels within the organization to want to do their best, not because of fear of their bosses, but because they want to perform well. It is that emotional commitment to quality at the sharp end that leaders of the future will have to develop.

Customers are becoming more demanding and increasingly diverse. This has led to an increasing tendency towards a 'win–win' partnership approach rather than the traditional 'win–lose' confrontational approach that has often been the style of carrying out business negotiations in the past.

These trends affect all levels within organizations and to date we have tended to accept that leadership is different at different levels. At the first line level we often talk about leadership episodes, a group of people being led towards a specific objective in a limited timescale with limited resources. This is what we call 'command task' leadership and it still has its place in leadership selection and training. Ambient leadership is about creating an environment, setting the day-to-day culture of the organization. The main trend in leadership style here in recent years has been the shift in the manager from boss to coach in terms of developing people in the organization. At the third and more strategic level we see leadership as a process of moving the whole organization forward. This process is the key to understanding a fundamental shift in leadership. In the next decade leadership will be concerned more with creating a process to pull people together and develop their ability to perform than with focusing on the qualities of one individual at whatever level they operate in the organization. It is this process of tapping into human potential which will differentiate the new-style leader from the old.

Effective Leadership for the Future

Effective leadership in the future will make use of the process of empowerment, with followers seeking empowerment rather than being tightly controlled. Effective leaders will understand the importance of aligning people with the organizational mission and they will encourage the creation of team goals to tap into potential abilities and performance levels. There will be more of a focus on competence at all levels within the organization and people will be given the freedom to act and, furthermore, will want to act on their own initiative. With enhanced performance levels being required from everybody, a recognition of stress in the workplace, as an aspect to be addressed and countered, will become commonplace. Accordingly, the skills of managing pressure will become accepted as a basic area of competence.

It used to be argued that the competencies required of an old-style first line supervisor were different from those needed by a main board director. While this is still going to be true in part, bearing in mind a probable shift in job titles, the main impact of changes in our organizations, such as delayering, is that first line-level leaders will need to be more aware of the strategic viewpoint and have a wider perspective, rather than simply focusing on their own part of the organization. At the same time, boards of directors will need to learn to work together as a team much more effectively than they have tended to in the past. This development is a major issue which will have an impact on some old-style leaders: it is vital that our leaders of the future retain and develop their ability to learn. Just as we are now promoting 'the learning organization', we need to promote 'the learning leader'. The board-room is the last stronghold to be breached by the corporate trainer, perhaps because directors seem to feel that training and development is meant for lower levels in the organization, not for the individuals at the top.

If we accept the premise that leadership is shifting from focus on the individual to creating a group or team process, we really do need to do more to develop the ability of the senior teams of our organizations in terms of a range of issues, from corporate governance to basic 'people skills'. In organizations, people tend to follow what they see in the way of behaviour from the people at the top. Individuals who have risen to the top in organizations cannot afford to ignore their position as powerful role models. As such, they need to be aware of how they affect other people and this involves them being part of an ongoing development programme in the same way as everyone else in the organization.

The process of learning to empower others is also important. Speed of response to the customer is a key issue for most organizations, whether from the public or private sector, service or manufacturing, and there is simply not enough time for decisions to be relayed up a hierarchy to the person at the top. Leaders will have to let go of some authority to enable their front line staff to respond rapidly to customer needs. This places another demand on the leader: it will no longer be acceptable for him or her to simply deploy individuals to do work as they are told. Leaders will need to devote a considerable amount of their time developing individual and group competence in order to ensure that the followers are equal to the demands being placed on them. In addition, the role of the leader in aligning the organization and ensuring that the mission, vision and values are communicated effectively to all levels of the organization, is going to be of prime importance.

In the future, leaders will understand that to be effective they will have to be holistic in their operation. They will need to understand more about the nature of human beings and operate at all the levels shown in the model of the individual presented in Figure 5.1. As this model shows, individuals have a sense of personal identity and, in order to be effective, leaders will need to link this sense of identity to the organization and to the team. People are more emotionally driven by their beliefs and values than we realize and effective leaders will understand how to shift people's beliefs from limiting ones to empowering ones. There will be more of an emphasis on aligning values in the organization, so that the capability of the organization can be increased as people focus their energy on the corporate mission rather than on internal politics.

People can only tap into their own capability if they are able to manage the pressure of their workload: if their 'state management' is efficient. Effective leaders of the future will understand that people who feel good about themselves produce good work, and so there will be more of an emphasis on creating a healthy culture in the organization and 'positive states' for the individuals. It is the state a person is in which determines their behaviour and what impact they have on their environment. The truly holistic leader will understand that, to get the best out of people, there is a requirement to operate simultaneously at all these levels: identity, beliefs and values, capability, state, behaviour and environment.

Mitel Telecom: Case Study

A good example of a company which has adapted these principles in order to achieve a significant change in a short period is Mitel, the telecommunication company. It is an interesting case because the management had the courage to take some very radical decisions, and because the impact on the 'bottom line' has been impressive.

Mitel was founded in Canada in 1972, and opened up in the UK in 1978. BT bought 51 per cent of the shares in 1986 when the turnover was $250 million. This looked a good investment for both companies but, two years later, having taken a decision to concentrate on core business, BT announced its intention to sell off Mitel within three years. Managing Director Alan Kirkham recalls that this was a period of considerable worry that tested everyone's resolve. Salvation came in the form of Schroder Ventures (a venture capitalist company) who bought out BT shares in 1991. They were content for Mitel management to run the company in their own way; two years later the turnover had risen to $400 million, and the company had moved to South Wales. By 1995, the turnover was $600 million and Schroder Ventures had reduced their share to 7 per cent.

On the surface, this looks like a good business success story, but Kirkham was not satisfied. Despite the timely intervention of Schroder Ventures in 1991 and the subsequent rise in turnover, he and the board knew that this was only a short-term gain. By 1993, the financial facts were clear: with expenses rising and prices being driven down by the recession, they had to do something radically different or the company would not survive in the longer term.

The board had taken careful note of the failures of the previous two years and developed a new Three-Year Plan aimed at doubling sales and trebling profits in the UK, based on a three-part strategy: diversification, process orientation and competitive advantage through people. The three parts were considered to be of equal importance and interdependent. The first two strategies are not particularly pertinent to this chapter, except that they were developed from a realization that business process re-engineering had not really worked and the diversification was to be directed into an entirely new family of products (away from telecommunications and into computers) with the intention of dominating sectors of the UK market.

The third strategy (competitive advantage through people) deserves analysis because of the radical decisions taken and the speed with which the strategy was implemented. Once the decision had been taken on the new Three-Year Plan, senior management spent six months communicating with everyone in the company. The message was clear and was reinforced repeatedly: (1) Mitel had to change – 'business as usual' was no longer an option; (2) no jobs for life – but instead lifetime employment opportunities for those with the appropriate skills; (3) Mitel would re-educate the workforce for a new 'process-oriented world', developing team-building and behavioural skills.

The result of this painstaking communication exercise was that the company only lost 60 people from a total workforce of 850. The majority of those who left took early retirement or decided, for whatever reason, that they did not want to be part of the new organization. In October 1994, the company changed – over a weekend! Kirkham justified this decision by saying, 'I didn't believe we could cross the chasm step-by-step. TQM was groaning under bureaucracy; the process was very fragmented and therefore too complex. Besides, the customers were not satisfied, so there was an excellent opportunity to change – completely' (interview with author, 2 November 1995). The top management had assembled evidence of best practice from a combination of gurus and customers, and then applied what was appropriate to Mitel. The significant features of the process were as follows:

- the hierarchical triangle was inverted, with the leader providing support as necessary,
- the number off managers was reduced from 70 to seven – over a weekend,
- seven tiers of management were removed – over a weekend,
- the company was reorganized into 11 business teams,
- the power of veto from top management was removed,
- job descriptions were burnt,
- facilitators from both inside and outside the company were employed,
- a programme of education for all employees was developed.

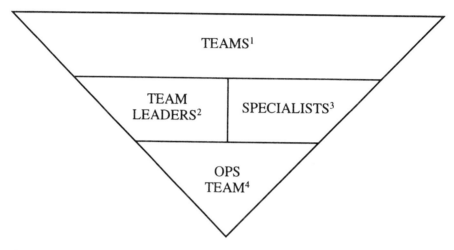

Notes:
1   11 customer-facing teams (all separate business).
2   Team leaders are facilitators (leadership is respected as a skill – like any other).
3   Specialists: process champions, skills champions.
4   Only seven in the Ops Team (formerly the board); they 'drive' the business: 50 per cent of their time taken with measuring and supporting the business, 50 per cent of their time taken with opportunity management.

Figure 8.1   Mitel's organizational structure

The new organizational structure is shown in Figure 8.1.
    Alan Kirkham is quite clear about the leadership issues:

leadership is about winning the hearts and minds of the people, based on behaviour and an open approach. I encourage everyone to contribute to any team – anywhere. We have mobile offices (which have removed barriers) and meeting rooms with Nobo boards which enable people to form ad hoc teams at any time. The result has been an impressive improvement in creativity, providing the company with competitive advantage due to the speed of innovation and production. (Interview with author, 2 November 1995)

Inverting the triangle has enabled the MD to react quickly to the customer via the business teams which are supported by the team leader, specialists and the Ops Team. For his part, he both facilitates those above him and keeps a close eye on direction and the process (helped by the fact that the business process has been reduced to a matrix on one sheet of paper).

The outcome is impressive. The company achieved a modest profit above target in the first 12 months. In the subsequent five months, however, they had exceeded the first twelve months' targets and had achieved month on month records for five out of the seven indicators.

This case provides clear evidence of what can be achieved through a radical approach, careful planning, clear communications, empowerment and democratic leadership. What is more, the business has benefited considerably by both a rapid improvement in the profits and a rejuvenated workforce who are now fully involved in the business. Alan Kirkham and his team have shown what can be achieved by embracing this new approach to leadership and it is possible that they will be followed by countless organizations in the next few years as people come to realize what is required to meet the challenge of the next century.

Blueprint for the Future

This section provides a guideline in preparation for the challenge identified above. We have considered future trends earlier in this chapter and have also looked at leadership competencies in Chapter 7. From this examination it is evident that the leadership skills for the new millennium will build on these competencies and will embrace the following:

- creating a vision,
- technological awareness,
- interpersonal relationships,
- systems thinking,
- developing and coaching people,
- developing teams.

Creating a vision that can be translated into reality requires leaders to have a wide view of their operation and related issues. Cross-functional training and, indeed, cross-industry and transnational training and experience have a significant role to play in this respect. Leaders who remain with a company and who are developed through that organization, avoiding any form of mind-broadening experience (including secondments) are likely to be narrow-minded and will be ill-equipped to deal with the unpredictability of the future.

No leaders of the future can afford to be technically ignorant. They will need both to be aware of the contribution that technology can make and to encourage its application where it will add value. We will not need leaders who are 'computer nerds', who surf the Internet instead of dealing with people. However, our leaders will need to be technologically aware and to keep abreast of developments.

The 'people skills' will become even more important than in the past. Leading by example, creating respect rather than distance, will become a major issue. More than ever before, leaders will need the ability to understand the impact on every part of the organization when they make changes, even minor ones. Organizations are now becoming so complex that nothing occurs in isolation. Even minor changes can have significant consequences both inside and outside the organization. Leaders will have to have a sound awareness of the systems impact of any of their leadership actions. Developing and coaching other people will also become very important in the move towards proper empowerment. Human resource is the most valuable yet least developed asset at our disposal. The added value that an effectively led individual can add to the operation of the organization can be tremendous. Leaders in the future will need to be even more effective at triggering this contribution.

Much work has been carried out in terms of creating and developing teams, and yet the issue of team leadership (leadership as a shared team function) is still in its infancy. The leader of the future will have to develop the ability to get other people to create an effective leadership process, particularly when operating as a team. The increasing complexity of work, the trend towards remoteness and empowerment will all place greater emphasis on team work (as in the case of Mitel).

Given such an environment, how do we select and develop the leaders of the future? In an era of constant change, how do we identify and nurture the talent required to lead people through change successfully? This is not easy. In many organizations, people are hampered by limiting beliefs about themselves, the organization, the management and the economy. The job of the effective leader of the future will be to become aware of these limiting beliefs, particularly the corporate ones, and to do something about changing them.

Above all, nurturing leadership for the future is about developing competence and confidence over a period of time. In effect, what is required is a continual leadership development (CLD) programme. This is similar to management development programmes arranged for their personnel by a number of companies or, for the individual, the Continuing Professional Development Guide provided by the Institute of Management in the UK. The latter model will become increasingly more appropriate as portfolio management becomes more the norm, resulting in individuals having to take responsibility for their own development rather than relying on career development being initiated by organizations.

The following blueprint considers both the corporate and individual programmes, as appropriate, set against the requirements for a CLD programme. It also takes account of the fact that we are now in the composite approach to leadership development whereby the theory and practice of leadership are interwoven over the lifetime of an individual.

Recruitment

Given that we are now in a period of constant change, and the key factor of leadership is managing change, organizations need to identify leadership potential at selection. It could be argued that this is done already by some organizations, by implication, when interviewing individuals for junior management positions or management trainee schemes. However, for the most part this is not done overtly, with the result that leadership potential (as opposed to management potential) is not assessed properly. This will need to be addressed in the future if organizations want to identify those individuals who are most likely to lead them through change successfully.

Interestingly, for a number of years now, the armed forces in Britain have identified leadership potential at selection. With regard to officers, they concentrate on those with leadership potential at the junior level, to meet the immediate requirement, but they also take a keen interest in those who appear to have a capacity for leadership at the higher level, eventually. Indeed, unless the individual shows leadership potential, he or she will not be selected for training. This is because the armed forces are quite clear that it is leadership that they require from their people. Exactly the same point is being confronted by their civilian counterparts as they face a world of constant change.

Developing Leadership Potential

For organizations, once they have identified the required characteristic at selection, there is the need to develop the potential. For the individual, there is also a requirement to develop skills and confidence.

All companies should include some form of leadership and team training during induction. This can either be done in-house or by using outside resources. The aim should be to begin developing leadership competencies, a clear understanding of self and also of the interaction of individuals within a team, right from the start. For organizations, all subsequent management development programmes should include leadership and team training tailored to meet the requirement of the individual and the organization. This needs to be progressive and developed together by the individual and the line manager as part of the appraisal system.

For those operating on their own, or with a portfolio lifestyle, developing a CLD is more difficult to achieve, especially if they are moving from job to job. However, use of the appraisal system when with a firm, combined with continuing advice from a mentor, can achieve a satisfactory result. Indeed, the constant monitoring of an individual's development by an independent mentor who is attached to an individual, as opposed to an organization, is likely to become an increasing trend for those living a portfolio lifestyle.

For both organizations and the individual, the development programmes will include a combination of courses on specific leadership skills, action learning, practical experience, coaching, mentoring, private reading and peer-group networking. The CLD programme needs to be holistic and aggressive: a mixture of programmed learning and practical experience, of action and reflection – all carefully monitored by an experienced mentor.

Senior Management

Those with the potential for senior management need to be carefully nurtured so that, when they rise to the strategic level, they have the confidence and competence to operate in that environment. There will only be a small percentage of such individuals and, of those with the potential, only a few will actually reach the top. There are a number of reasons for the failure to realize potential, which can include such varying factors as burnout, a loss of confidence or a reassessment of personal priorities (such as putting the family before the job). However, it is crucial to ensure that someone who is likely to be incompetent at the strategic level is not appointed to such a position. Failures at the strategic level tend to be catastrophic and have far-reaching implications throughout an organization. Sadly, there are a number of examples of failure at the top level, and these are likely to increase in the complex workplace of tomorrow unless individuals are carefully prepared for leadership at the strategic level.

The senior management development programme needs to be a rigorous exposure of practical experience and programmed learning. The practical experience should consist of a series of testing appointments designed to enable the individual to gather experience and develop a personal style to deal with complex issues under pressure. They should be encouraged to take risks, be creative and develop the skill to lead high-quality teams. Feedback needs to be open and honest, and the challenge should be raised appropriately until the coach is satisfied that the individual is ready in all aspects to operate competently at the strategic level.

Programme learning can be provided either in-house or from an outside resource. Whichever is chosen, it is essential that individuals are exposed to new ideas, other cultures and radical thinking: it is the development of the holistic approach which is sought. One such programme is the Postgraduate Diploma/Masters in Leadership at the University of Exeter. The course was established in 1993 and is designed to assist organizations to develop the leadership of selected individuals. The Diploma is a part-time programme and consists of 7 one-week modules spread over two years. Course members participate in practical exercises, are exposed to the spectrum of leadership theory (including those of the current gurus), other cultures and learn from successful, established leaders from both the public and private sectors. This pioneering course, which is the only one of its type in Europe, has demonstrated that preparation for strategic leadership can be developed immensely over such a time frame. Furthermore, the mixing of representatives from large and small organizations is both stimulating and interesting due to the different perspectives offered. Course members are encouraged to develop radical ideas and challenged to put forward their own thoughts, which are often tested in a practical setting. They also have the opportunity, between modules, to apply in their own organizations what they learn on the programme. Not surprisingly, they grow significantly in confidence and competence as their course progresses.

More such programmes are required if we are to develop the strategic leaders we need for the future. As a minimum, any senior management programme should include the following:

- the skill of creating a vision,
- strategic leadership,
- innovation,
- leading multicultural and international teams,
- communication skills at the top,
- public relations,
- crisis management,
- how to get the best from people,
- understanding oneself,
- how to lead high-performance teams.

There is one other aspect of senior management development which requires comment – secondments. In the past there has been a tendency for the high-fliers to stay within the corporate environment so that they can climb relentlessly up the hierarchical ladder. One of the benefits of the flattening of structures is that there are fewer rungs on the ladder and therefore more chances for secondments. These openings should be seized only by those individuals with aspirations towards strategic leadership, since exposure to other cultures is one of the best learning opportunities available. The significance lies in the relationship between the length of time spent in a single culture and conservatism. The longer an individual remains with one organization, the more conservative he or she becomes. Quite often, the only means of breaking the mould is a period away from the organization, which forces the individual to look at affairs afresh, and from a different perspective. Not only can this be a stimulating experience, it also usually leads to the individual having the confidence to try a different and radical approach when returning to the parent organization.

It is this willing attitude towards creativity, lateral thinking and challenge to the status quo which is crucial at the strategic level. This needs to be developed via a CLD programme or secondment or, preferably, both.

Summary

A CLD programme needs to be flexible, progressive and tailored to the individual's requirements. For organizations, this will probably involve a mixture of in-house programmes, external courses and practical experience. For the individual, it will require a determination to take responsibility for their own development. For the providers, it will require a flexible approach in order to meet customer needs. Increasingly, this is likely to be in the form of a modular programme to match portfolio lifestyles and enable partici-pants to fit this into a very busy schedule.

Given the relationship between leadership and change, a CLD programme will become an essential management process for those with aspirations to become leaders at the strategic level. Organizations will need to provide such a programme for their core high-fliers if they want to keep them. Otherwise, the talented will be tempted to join the majority pursuing a portfolio lifestyle.

Conclusion

As we approach an uncertain, exciting future it is becoming clear that the requirement for leadership is shifting. It is not changing completely, since many of the old principles remain as strong as ever – values, integrity, setting an example, setting direction, getting the best out of people, communication – but there is evidence of a subtle shift of emphasis which is now emerging. In many ways, the renewed interest in leadership has served to reinforce the old-fashioned values and it has also forced people to examine how to adapt to future needs.

'The future' is developing at a breakneck pace as we enter a new age of constant change and increasing complexity. Developing technology, new, more flexible ways of work, moves towards remote management and portfolio lifestyle will all pose considerable challenges to tomorrow's leaders, and it is already clear that not enough is being done to prepare people for this chaotic environment.

As part of the debate to determine the way forward, this book has sought to find a practical course of action. As the emphasis focuses on the individual during the last years of the twentieth century, so people will need to know more about themselves and how they react with others in a team. We believe that this is an essential competence for tomorrow's leaders, who will be much more plentiful than today since they will be operating at all levels.

We foresee dilemmas: when to switch from a 'soft' approach to a 'hard' decision; when to move from empowerment to a directive approach; when to rely on intuition. We believe that in time, intuition will become a recognized competence as leaders wrestle with increasing complexities, a situation which highlights the pressing need for leadership at the strategic level: the ability to lead teams of experts to solve complex issues.

The leaders of tomorrow need help and guidance if they are to succeed in the future. The move towards empowerment, remoteness and reliance on technology contains a diversity of leadership challenges which have not been faced before. There is an acute need to provide the resources to facilitate the training and development of leaders at all levels. Leaders will have to be more competent than ever before if they are to meet the challenges of the twenty-first century; they will need to be flexible enough to grow and develop as the situations which they are required to handle, change. In effect, we are entering the Age of the Learning Leader.

Bibliography

Adair, J. (1983), *Effective Leadership*, London: Pan.

Adair, J. (1988), *Training for Leadership*, Aldershot: Gower.

Adair, J. (1989), *Great Leaders*, Guildford: Talbot Adair Press.

Bandler, R. (1985), *Using Your Brain – for a CHANGE*, Utah: Real People Press.

Bandler, R. and MacDonald, W. (1988), *An Insider's Guide to Submodalities*, California: Meta Publications.

Bass, B.M. (1990), *Bass & Stogdill's Handbook of Leadership*, New York: The Free Press.

Belbin, M. (1981), *Management Teams: Why They Succeed or Fail*, Oxford: Butterworth–Heinemann.

Belbin, M. (1993), *Team Roles at Work*, Oxford: Butterworth–Heinemann.

Belbin, M. (1996), *The Coming Shape of Organisation*, Oxford: Butterworth–Heinemann.

Bennis, W. (1989), *On Becoming A Leader*, London: Century Business.

Bion, W.R. (1991), *Experiences In Groups*, London: Routledge.

Blake, R.R. and Mouton, J.S. (1964), *The Managerial Grid*, Houston: Gulf Publishing.

Briggs Myers, I. (1962), *Introduction to Type*, Palo Alto, California: Consulting Psychologists Press.

Briggs Myers, I. (1985), *Guide to the Development and Use of the Myers Briggs Type Indicator*, Palo Alto, California: Consulting Psychologist Press.

Carlzon, J. (1989), *Moments of Truth*, New York: Harper Collins.

Carnegie, D. and Associates (1993), *The Leader In You*, New York: Simon & Schuster.

Cooper C.L. Cooper, R.D. and Eaker, L.H. (1991), *Living with Stress*, Harmondsworth: Penguin.

Covey, S.R. (1989), *The Seven Habits of Highly Effective People*, New York: Simon & Schuster.

Curtis, A. (1994), 'How to be Productive', *Professional Manager*, March.

Dixon, N.F. (1976), *On the Psychology of Military Incompetence*, London: Jonathan Cape.

Dobson, M. and Wakelem, R. (1993), *Management Structure & Organisation – The Lesson of the Recession*, Exeter University.

Eccles, R.G. and Nohria, N. (1992), *Beyond the Hype*, Boston: Harvard Business School Press.

Fiedler, F.E., Chemers, M. and Mahar, L. (1976), *Improving Leadership Effectiveness: The Leader Match Concept*, New York: Wiley.

Fisher, K. (1993), *Leading Self-Directed Work Teams*, New York: McGraw-Hill.

Forgas, J. (1979), *Social Episodes*, European Association of Experimental Social Psychology, in association with Academic Press.

Gardner, H. (1996), *Leading Minds: An Anatomy of Leadership*, London: Harper Collins.

Garratt, B. (1994), *The Learning Organisation*, London: Harper Collins.

Hamel, G. and Prahalad, C.K. (1994), *Competing for the Future*, Boston: Harvard Business School Press.

Handy, C. (1985), *The Future of Work*, Oxford: Blackwell.

Handy, C. (1985), *Understanding Organisations*, Harmondsworth: Penguin.

Handy, C. (1990), *The Age of Unreason*, London: Arrow.

Handy, C. (1994), *The Empty Raincoat*, London: Hutchinson.

Heller, R. (1995), 'The Heart of the Quality Matter', *Management Today*, June.

Hersey, P. and Blanchard, K.H. (1969), *Management of Organizational Behavior*, Englewood Cliffs, NJ: Prentice-Hall.

Holmes, T.H. and Rahe, R.H. (1967), 'The Social Readjustment Rating Scale', *Journal of Psychosomatic Research*, **2**, (2).

Hughes, R.L., Ginnett, R.C. and Curphy, G.J. (1996), *Leadership: Enhancing the Lessons of Experience*, Chicago: Irwin.

Jaques, E. and Cason, K. (1994), *Human Capability*, Falls Church, VA: Cason Hall.

Jaques, E. and Clement, S. (1991), *Executive Leadership*, Oxford: Blackwell.

Jung, C.G. (1971), *Psychological Types, Bollinger Series XX The Collected Works of C.G. Jung*, Vol. 6, Princeton: Princeton University Press.

Kanter, R.M. (1983), *The Change Masters*, New York: Simon & Schuster.

Katzenbach, J.R. and Smith, D.K. (1993), *The Wisdom of Teams*, Boston: Harvard Business School Press.

Kirk, D. (1992), 'World-class Teams', *The McKinsey Quarterly*, No. 4.

Kotter, J.P. (1990), *A Force for Change*, New York: The Free Press.

Margerison, C. and McCann, D. (1990), *Team Management*, London: Mercury Books.

Mayor, F. (1995), *The New Page*, Aldershot: Dartmouth.

O'Connor, J. and Seymour, J. (1990), *Introducing Neuro-Linguistic Programming*, London: Mandala.

Peters, T.J. (1987), *Thriving on Chaos*, London: Macmillan.

Peters, T.J. (1994), *The Tom Peters Seminar*, New York: Vintage Books.

Peters, T.J. and Waterman, R.H. (1982), *In Search of Excellence*, New York: Harper & Row.

Robbins, A. (1988), *Unlimited Power*, London: Simon & Schuster.

Robbins, A. (1992), *Awaken the Giant Within*, London: Simon & Schuster.

Rogers, C. (1969), *On Becoming a Person*, London: Constable.

RSA Inquiry (1995), *Tomorrow's Company*, London: Royal Society of Arts.

Sashkin, M. (1986), *How to Become a Visionary Leader*, Bryn Mawr, PA: Organization Design and Development Inc.

Semler, R. (1993), *Maverick*, London: Century.

Senge, P.M. (1993), *The Fifth Discipline*, London: Century Business.

Senge, P.M. *et al.* (1994), *The Fifth Discipline Fieldbook*, London: Nicholas Brealey Publishing Limited.

Shackleton, Viv. (1995), *Business Leadership*, London: Routledge.

Stogdill, R.M. (1974), *Handbook of Leadership: A Survey of Theory and Research*, London: Macmillan.

Syrett, M. and Hogg, C. (eds) (1992), *Frontiers Of Leadership*, Oxford: Blackwell.

Trompenaars, F. (1993), *Riding the Waves of Culture*, London: Economist Books.

Warr, P. (1993), *Training for Managers*, London: Institute of Managers.

Whiteley, R.C. (1991), *The Customer Driven Company*, London: Century.

Continual leadership development

Anyone who would like further advice with Continual Leadership Development can contact either of the authors at the following addresses:

Alan Hooper: Director
                Centre for Leadership Studies
                University of Exeter
                Crossmead
                Barley Lane
                Exeter, England
                EX4 1TF, UK

John Potter: John Potter International Consulting
                PO Box 21
                Dartmouth
                Devon, England
                TQ6 0YA, UK

Index